Deutsche Grammophon: State of the Art

CELEBRATING OVER A CENTURY OF MUSICAL EXCELLENCE

RIZZOLI
NEW YORK

New York · Paris · London · Milan

First published in the United States of America in 2010 by
Rizzoli International Publications, Inc.
300 Park Avenue South
New York, NY 10010
www.rizzoliusa.com

Originally published in 2009 by
Verlhac Editions
8 rue Lincoln
75008 Paris
France
www.verlhaceditions.com

© 2009 Verlhac Editions
© Text (in order of appearance): Rémy Louis, Thierry Soveaux, and Olivier Boruchowitch
© Captions: Yannick Coupannec and Rémy Louis
Picture research: Yannick Coupannec
Interviews and testimonials: compiled by Olivier Boruchowitch
Design: Sophie Baillot
Translation: Anne McDowall, Jochen Rudelt, Margarete Schubert, John Tyler Tuttle, and Eva Zöllner

2010 2011 2012 2013 / 10 9 8 7 6 5 4 3 2 1

ISBN: 978-0-8478-3531-7

Library of Congress Control Number: 2010923812

Printed in China

Deutsche Grammophon: State of the Art

CELEBRATING OVER A CENTURY OF MUSICAL EXCELLENCE

TEXT **RÉMY LOUIS, THIERRY SOVEAUX, AND OLIVIER BORUCHOWITCH**
ICONOGRAPHY **YANNICK COUPANNEC**

RIZZOLI
NEW YORK

New York · Paris · London · Milan

"With 111 years of history behind it, Deutsche Grammophon remains the world's largest and proudest classical music label. Since its 100th anniversary eleven years ago, it has continued to thrive in an especially challenging global environment for recorded music. In nearly two decades of leading the worldwide classical music business for Universal Music, it has been a huge but rewarding challenge to help guide this great label into the future. Deutsche Grammophon continues to flourish because it has never lost sight of its underlying philosophy: support the artist with the means to make great music and deliver this great music to the public in a beautiful package with creative ideas."

CHRISTOPHER ROBERTS

President, Classics and Jazz
Universal Music Group International

TABLE OF CONTENTS

[01]

STATE OF THE ART
THE STORY OF DEUTSCHE GRAMMOPHON
1898–1945

RÉMY LOUIS

Deutsche Grammophon, a pioneering and key player in the story of recorded music, celebrated its centenary in 1998. In commemorating its 111th anniversary in 2009, the label can pride itself on a history that spans three centuries. However, it was not its German founder, Emile Berliner (1851–1929), who was the first to invent a way of recording sound. The credit for that goes to Frenchman Charles Cros, though his proposal of April 30, 1877, was never developed. On December 19 of the same year, American Thomas Edison registered a patent that led, in 1878, to the creation of the first "talking machine," which he christened the phonograph. This was the first machine capable of reproducing speech, which was Edison's initial goal. It was in 1877, too, that Berliner invented a microphone, which he sold—patented and improved—to the Bell Telephone Company, the firm founded by Alexander Graham Bell. The inventor of the telephone perfected the phonograph before selling the rights to the design to a consortium that founded the American Gramophone Company in 1887. Meanwhile, Berliner, who had by that time returned to Hanover (he had emigrated to the United States in 1870), continued his research, which culminated in the invention of a system that differed from Edison's.

THE BIRTH OF RECORDING

In simple terms, the goal of sound recording is to transcribe the vibration produced by a sound emission onto a storage medium and then to mechanically read and amplify this vibration to reproduce the sound. The recording process can be summarized as follows: the sound source causes the vibration of a membrane; this vibration is then transmitted to a stylus, which inscribes an undulating groove. To reproduce the sound, a stylus follows this groove, picking up the vibration and transmitting it to a membrane that plays back the sound. Thus sound is stored in a material form similar—"analog"—to the vibration to which it corresponds. In essence, this technique for recording sound remained unchanged until the advent of digital recording and the compact disc (CD), but it was constantly being improved over its century-long history.

The recording device invented by Edison consisted of a wax cylinder with grooves inscribed in a spiral around the outer surface. The process suffered from two limitations: firstly, the engraving system, perpendicular to the surface of the cylinder, allowed the stylus to make only an up-and-down movement into the wax (known as the "hill and dale" process); secondly, it was virtually impossible to cast these cylinders, which limited their distribution. Berliner perfected the process, solving both these problems: his invention, the phonographic disc, had a lateral groove inscribed in a spiral, and the stylus vibrated from right to left within the groove. Not only did the disc wear out much less quickly than Edison's cylinder, but it could also be pressed and duplicated by electrotyping, a process that enables metal matrices to be cast from a soft-wax original. Like genuine molds, these matrices could then be used to press the required number of discs. This first disc, made of zinc and 12 cm in diameter, turned at a speed of 150 rpm, and recorded just one minute of sound on its single side. Berliner also devised the machine that read these phonographic discs, which he named the gramophone. The phonographic disc and gramophone together were patented on September 29, 1887.

Thus Berliner brought the work of art into the age of mechanical reproduction, to borrow the title of philosopher Walter Benjamin's famous essay. He presented his machine to the Franklin Institute in Philadelphia on May 16, 1888. A patent war then began between Bell, Edison, and Berliner. Determined to exploit his invention (Edison's phonograph was already well ahead), Berliner presented it in Germany in 1889. The following year, he granted toy manufacturer Kämmerer & Reinhardt the license to produce his manually operated record player. From that moment, he was on his way to becoming the first record tycoon. In fact, he was already an industrialist, having founded the Berliner Telephonfabrik, the first factory in Europe specializing in the manufacture of telephone equipment, with his brothers Joseph and Manfred, in 1881. The factory was established in Hanover, the Berliners' native city (first in Kniestrasse, then, from 1904, in Podbielskistrasse). In 1893 Berliner founded the United States Gramophone Company in Washington and hired Fred Gaisberg, who became the first, if not the greatest, classical music producer in the history of recording.

While continuing his research into the material composition of the record (a mixture of lac, mineral powder, lampblack, and vegetable fibers to ensure a quality pressing), Berliner sought to establish his business financially. This he managed to do, with some difficulty, in 1895, thanks to the Pennsylvania Railroad Company: on October 8, he founded the Berliner Gramophone Company. The following year, Eldridge R. Johnson designed the spring motor, which did away with the need to manually crank a handle to operate the gramophone. He joined Berliner, along with Frank Seaman, who founded the National Gramophone Company, to distribute and promote the records and equipment produced by Berliner. The specification of the record had evolved slightly: it was now 17 cm in diameter, had a playing time of 90 seconds, and rotated at a speed of 70 rpm, which was increased to 78.26 rpm when the first electric motor appeared.

[03]

[05]

Kaiserliches Patentamt

KAISERLICHES PATENTAMT.

AUSGEGEBEN DEN 2. NOVEMBER 1888.

PATENTSCHRIFT

— № 45048 —

KLASSE 21: ELEKTRISCHE APPARATE.

EMILE BERLINER IN WASHINGTON (COLUMBIA, V. ST. A.).

Verfahren und Apparat für das Registriren und Wiederhervorbringen von Tönen.

Patentirt im Deutschen Reiche vom 8. November 1887 ab.

[02]

[04]

[01] German Emile Berliner (1851–1929) inspecting one of his first records, Berlin, 1889.

[02] American Thomas Alva Edison (1847–1931), the inventor of the phonograph, photographed in his study.

[03] One of the first (and most basic) models of Edison's phonograph, circa 1878.

[04] A view of the Berliner "Telephonfabrik" in Hanover, the first factory in Europe to specialize in manufacturing telephone equipment, owned by the Berliner brothers.

[05] From left to right: Emile, Joseph, and Manfred Berliner.

[06] A drawing by Emile Berliner for his patent for the gramophone, registered in November 1887 in Washington.

[07] Fred Gaisberg (1873–1951), the first classical music producer in the history of recording. He personally financed the first recordings of the famous singer Caruso.

[07]

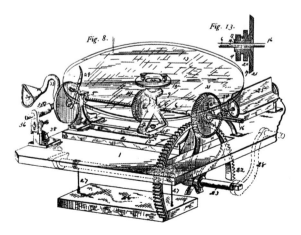

Fig. 13.

Fig. 8.

[06]

While these developments were taking place, Berliner was battling those who were trying to get a foothold in the fledgling market, through forgeries if necessary. In 1898, along with his associate William Berry Owen, he founded the Gramophone Company in London, where Gaisberg continued as producer. Success quickly followed, but Seaman's split with Berliner and Johnson provoked a crisis. Gaisberg went to Hanover to ensure that the recordings made in London could be pressed in Hanover. The testing, which was conclusive, was undertaken in a hangar.

THE BEGINNINGS OF AN INDUSTRY

On December 6, 1898, the Berliner brothers' Deutsche Grammophon Gesellschaft mbH was incorporated (translated from English to German, "gramophone" loses its "e" but gains an "m"), a private limited company with a capital of 20,000 marks, to begin producing records. They imported the necessary hydraulic presses from the United States, while the Gramophone Company in England supplied the matrices. The venture was so successful that a subsidiary company, the Compagnie Française du Gramophone, was formed in France in 1899, and others soon followed it in Austria and Russia. By 1900 the Hanover factory had forty-five record presses in operation. On June 27, the company was reorganized into a simplified joint stock company, with a capital of 1,000,000 marks—a considerable sum at that time—with its administrative headquarters in Berlin. 40 percent of the shares of the company, which was associated with Orpheus Musikwerke GmbH in Leipzig, were held by the Berliner brothers, while the remaining 60 percent were held by the Gramophone Company in London, which soon took control of Deutsche Grammophon. The Hanover factory was thus in English ownership, which would not be without consequences for its future. The same year, Deutsche Grammophon chose as its emblem Francis Barraud's painting *His Master's Voice*, depicting a dog sitting in front of a horn. The trademark, registered on July 10, 1900, reproduced this soon-to-be famous painting, which made the fox terrier Nipper a worldwide celebrity. Translated into German (*Die Stimme seines Herrn*), it superseded the company's original trademark, the Recording Angel (*Schreibender Engel*), on record labels from 1909.

It was also in 1900, during the Boer War, that Gaisberg recorded a track that met with huge success: *The Departure of a Troop Ship* mixed the sounds of ships' sirens and women crying with the song "Home, Sweet Home." It is a perfect example of the often documentary nature of early recordings— marches, fanfares, and animal noises were the best sounds for disguising the background noise inherent in 78s! The lawsuit brought by Seaman in 1901 that removed the protected trademark status from the term *gramophone* had no serious repercussions. At that time, 5,000 tracks were being pressed "in every language in the world" and distributed throughout Europe, with much publicity ("hard disc record, no soft cylinders"). In 1901 the first 25 cm–diameter discs appeared; in 1903 the diameter was increased to 30 cm, which allowed five minutes of recording on a single side.

[09]

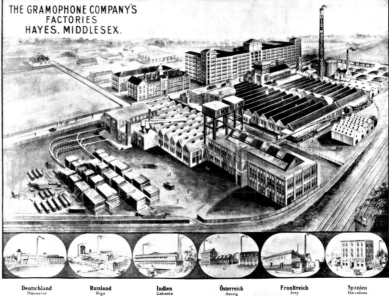

[11]

[10]

[08]

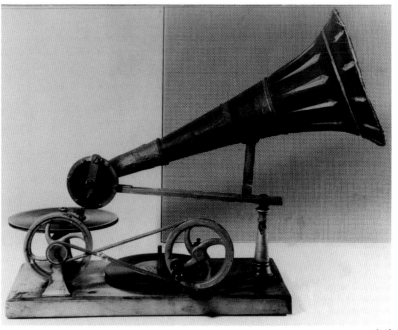

[08] Joseph Berliner and his workers in the hangar at Hanover where the first records were made, 1889.

[09] The staff of the Hanover factory, circa 1898.

[10] One of the first gramophone records, circa 1903. *The Recording Angel* was the label's original logo.

[11] The Gramophone Company's factory in Hayes, England, in 1912. The German subsidiary based in Hanover was then English owned. The French subsidiary was based in Ivry, on the outskirts of Paris.

[12] Berliner's gramophone: this model dates from 1889.

[12]

[13]

[14]

[15]

[13] A 1904 advertisement showing *The Recording Angel* trademark. It was replaced in 1909.

[14] An advertisement, circa 1904, for a gramophone with a horn. *The Recording Angel* is also visible here, in a slightly different design.

[15] Music and dance in the open air . . . or how to use the gramophone in unexpected ways!

[16]

[17]

[18]

[19]

[16]…[18] German advertisements from 1909/10, announcing the artists who could be heard on record. Note the portraits of Arthur Nikisch, Richard Strauss, Leo Blech, and Felix Weingartner, all key figures of the label.

[19] In 1909 *The Recording Angel* was superseded by the soon-to-be-legendary *"His Master's Voice"* logo, the reproduction of a painting by Francis Barraud, which introduced the fox terrier Nipper. Registered in 1900 by the English Gramophone Company, the trademark became *Die Stimme seines Herrn* in German, *La Voce del Padrone* in Italian, and *La voix de son maître* in French.

THE FIRST ARTIST CONTRACTS

However, artists needed to be convinced that records and recording were something more than just a flash in the pan, because Berliner and his associates perceived that, beyond recorded speech, songs, and medleys, records had incredible potential as a means of broadcasting art and culture. Feodor Chaliapin, in 1902, was the first to sign a contract, after fastidiously detailed negotiations. Superstitiously, he believed that recording would cause him to lose his voice; reportedly he would cross himself before each recording session, and it was not unheard of for him to stand bare-chested, like a boxer, in front of the pickup horn! Also in 1902, Enrico Caruso cut his first tracks in the Albergo Milano of Milan, in a room above the one in which Verdi had died in 1901. He demanded a fee of 100 pounds for recording ten opera arias; the Gramophone Company refused in a telegram that has become famous: "exorbitant fee, recording prohibited." Convinced that this was an error of historic magnitude, Gaisberg overrode the decision and paid the great tenor from his own purse. Over the following twenty years, Caruso's recordings brought in more than 3,000,000 pounds! Singers were already being attentively wooed: Antonio Scotti, Francesco Tamagno (the voice of Othello in Verdi's opera and the first artist to receive royalties), Leo Slezak, Mattia Battistini, Emma Calvé, and Luisa Tetrazzini, all internationally recognized, in turn cut their first records. So, too, in 1903, did Alessandro Moreschi, the last surviving castrato, whose voice allegedly resembled no other.

Records were first sold in toy and bicycle shops, before finding their ways into music bookshops and musical-instrument stores. The factory in Podbielskistrasse was expanded and was now dedicated exclusively to the manufacture of records; it could press 25,000 a day. Mary Garden, Elena Gerhardt, and Geraldine Farrar were added to the list of singers who were engaged, with inimitable discernment, by Gaisberg. Another new recruit was Nellie Melba, who admitted that it was *The Departure of a Troop Ship* that had convinced her, and confessed that her recordings won her offers of marriage from men who had never even seen her. Gaisberg discovered to his cost that divas can be capricious: he and his team waited several days at the whim of Adelina Patti, to whose Welsh castle they had traveled with all their equipment. But she was overjoyed with the result, and what followed measured up to all expectations: her seventeen marketed recordings beat all previous sales records. The company was named official supplier to the royal families of England and Spain, which its founder quite legitimately saw as an accolade.

Meanwhile, technology was evolving: one significant improvement was that, from 1907, both sides of a disc could be recorded. But perhaps most importantly, Deutsche Grammophon bought, from a company in Leipzig, the revolutionary patent for a record player without a horn, which was soon marketed under the name "Gramola." Two years later, the company opened shops selling records and record players (Grammophon Spezialhaus GmbH). The list grew constantly: following in the footsteps of violinists Joseph Joachim and Jan Kubelik and pianists Josef Hofmann and Alfred Grünfeld, German pianist Wilhelm Backhaus cut his first tracks, extracts from *The Well-Tempered Clavier*. In 1910 he was also the soloist for the first recording with an orchestra, the Allegro molto moderato from Grieg's Piano Concerto in A Minor, conducted by Landon Ronald. Another legendary musician who signed up in 1911 was the Polish pianist Ignace Jan Paderewski. Bruno Seidler-Winkler, also a pianist but first and foremost a conductor, recorded *Carmen* (with Emmy Destinn in the lead role) in 1908.

[21]

[22]

[20]

[24]

[20] Enrico Caruso (1873–1921) in the lead role in Giuseppe Verdi's opera *Ernani*. The most emblematic tenor of the twentieth century, Caruso made his first recording for the Gramophone Company in 1902.

[21] An example of one of many 78s recorded by Caruso: the title role's aria "*Un di, all'azzurro spazio*" from Umberto Giordano's *Andrea Chénier*.

[22] As well as being a great singer, Caruso was also a talented caricaturist, as shown in this humorous self-portrait of one of his recording sessions. His cartoons of Mahler and Toscanini are also well known.

[23] The legendary Russian bass Feodor Chaliapin (1873–1938), depicted here in the role of Mephistopheles, was also renowned for his exceptional acting ability.

[24] A poster for four "extraordinary performances" of Verdi's *Otello* at the Municipal Casino in Nice in 1887. Francesco Tamagno (1850–1905) had created the role of the Moor of Venice on February 5, 1887, at La Scala in Milan just a few days earlier!

[25]

ROUGE
fragrant with Parfum

Mary Garden

1. Lie de Vin (Dark)   6. Indian Blush
2. Vermilion Poppy   7. Vermeil
3. Egyptian Poppy   8. Lie de Vin (Medium)
4. Persian Blush   9. Light Rouge
5. Rosebud   10. Intense Brunette
           11. Deep Brunette

Rigaud
16 Rue de la Paix
·PARIS·

Geo Borgfeldt & Co.
Sole Distributors New York

[26]

PARFUM GERALDINE FARRAR
V. RIGAUD PARIS

PARFUM GERALDINE FARRAR
A delicate but lasting sublimation of the olfactory sensations inspired by the beauty of this charming artiste.

[27]

[28]

[25] Alessandro Moreschi (1858–1922) in 1880. Famous in history as "the last castrato," he was also the only one to be recorded.

[26] [27] Singers Geraldine Farrar (1882–1967) and Mary Garden (1874–1967) were the real stars of their time. It was therefore natural that the famous Parisian perfumer Rigaud, established in 1852, should use them to promote its perfumes and cosmetics.

[28] The Austrian tenor Leo Slezak (1873–1946) in the title role of Richard Wagner's opera *Tannhäuser*.

[29]

[30]

[31]

[29] The soprano Adelina Patti (1843–1919), photographed by Nadar.

[30] Nellie Melba (1861–1931): her already great fame grew even more widespread with her recordings, which won her many marriage proposals from admirers who had never seen her perform on stage. The French chef Escoffier created a now-famous dessert, the peach Melba, in her honor.

[31] The Czech soprano Emmy Destinn (1878–1930) in the title role of Georges Bizet's opera *Carmen*, which she recorded in 1908.

[32] … [35] German advertisements that appeared in 1912 to promote the new Gramola, the first record player without a horn. The shops selling these record players also sold the records. The middle-class elegance of the people they depict suggests that these record players were aimed primarily at a wealthy clientele.

[34]

[35]

[33]

[36]

[36] The Czech violinist Jan Kubelik (1880–1940) during a recording session, accompanied at the piano by Bruno Seidler-Winkler. Also a conductor and composer, Kubelik recorded *Carmen* with Emmy Destinn.

[37] Three great artists strike a pose: the German pianist Wilhelm Backhaus (1884–1969, seated), Leo Slezak (leaning on the piano), and the German violinist Willy Burmester (1869–1933), photographed in 1914.

[38] The legendary Polish pianist and composer Josef Hofmann (1876–1957), who later became a naturalized American, photographed in 1896.

[39] The Polish pianist Ignace Jan Paderewski (1860–1941), photographed in 1910. Paderewski had many strings to his bow: a pianist and celebrated composer, he was also a politician and high-ranking diplomat. In January 1919 he became prime minister and foreign minister of an independent Poland.

[37]

[38]

[39]

[40]

[41]

[42]

[40] A recording session of Wagner's *Parsifal* with the Berlin Philharmonic, conducted by the German maestro Alfred Hertz (1872–1942, with black beard, braces, and white shirt), who was then making a career for himself at the Metropolitan Opera in New York. Limited to symphonic extracts, the recording was the first made by the Berlin orchestra.

[41] [42] A few weeks later, the charismatic Hungarian conductor Arthur Nikisch (1855–1922) also made news when he made the first complete recording of Beethoven's Symphony no. 5. This is the English pressing of the recording.

In 1913 Deutsche Grammophon created a sensation when it released, on four double-sided 78s, the first complete recording of Beethoven's Symphony no. 5 in C Minor, an honor that was entrusted to the Berlin Philharmonic and its charismatic conductor Arthur Nikisch. A few weeks earlier, Alfred Hertz had recorded large symphonic extracts from Wagner's *Parsifal* with the Berlin Philharmonic. In recording the latter, Deutsche Grammophon had shown itself to be remarkably quick to act: until then, performance of the opera had been exclusively confined to Bayreuth, and the rights to perform this final work of Wagner's elsewhere had only just been released.

THE GERMAN DEUTSCHE GRAMMOPHON

The outbreak of World War I brought a brutal halt to this harmonious development (in 1908 production had reached an unsurpassed figure of 6,200,000 records). Military demands took precedence, and this meant a shortage of the lac, imported from India, that was an essential ingredient in record manufacture. Because of the shortfall in supplies, the company decided not to sell records except to those who brought back their old, unwanted ones! More seriously, the Reich government seized Deutsche Grammophon's assets on the pretext that, being English, the company belonged to the enemy. This forced requisition brought about the separation, in 1916, of the German and English branches of the company (the Gramophone Company became EMI in 1931 after merging with the Columbia Graphophone Company). Gaisberg stayed with the English branch. This change resulted in the share repurchase of the firm by Polyphon-Musikwerke of Leipzig the following year, which placed Deutsche Grammophon in a new situation. Manufacture dropped to 400,000 records in 1917, and in 1918, the Hanover firm was banned from using the *Die Stimme seines Herrn* trademark, which remained the property of the Gramophone Company. Suddenly, Caruso, Melba, Patti, Tita Ruffo, and Emma Calvé disappeared from the catalogue, and the sum of these losses proved a greater one. But what better solution to the problem than to draw from the pool of a whole new generation of German performers who were coming to maturity? This was particularly the case in Berlin, where musical life in the 1920s offered an unprecedented concentration of talent. The new company moved its head office there in 1918.

The leading baritone Heinrich Schlusnus was signed in 1916 and the composer Richard Strauss, then at the height of his career, in 1917. (The latter regularly recorded his works, including his lieder, from then on.) Alongside them were major artists, such as sopranos Maria Ivogün, Lotte Lehmann, Frida Leider, and Elisabeth Schumann; contralto Emmi Leisner; tenors Hermann Jadlowker, Tino Patticra, and Lauritz Melchior; bass Alexander Kipnis; violinists Fritz Kreisler, Mischa Elman, Georg Kulenkampff, and Carl Flesch; and pianists Eugen d'Albert, Raoul von Koczalski, and Wilhelm Kempff. (In 1920, the latter embarked on a relationship with Deutsche Grammophon that would last for sixty years, recording Beethoven's *Écossaises* and Bagatelle in C Major, op. 33, no. 2.) Hans Pfitzner, Max von Schillings, and Franz Schreker, all renowned composers, followed Strauss in recording with Deutsche Grammophon, though not exclusively their own works (Pfitzner, for example, was well-known as a conductor of Beethoven and Schumann). There were also recordings conducted by Hermann Abendroth, Leo Blech, Fritz Busch, and Oskar Fried. Meanwhile, the death knell sounded for the phonograph cylinder in 1918, and manufacture ceased. Hans B. Hasse made his first recordings and soon became one of the firm's great sound technicians, with a career lasting until the end of World War II.

[44]

[43] Photographed in 1920 during one of his first recording sessions, the German pianist Wilhelm Kempff (1895–1991) became a rare symbol of longevity and fidelity, having recorded for Deutsche Grammophon for more than fifty years.

[44] The baritone Heinrich Schlusnus (1888–1952), the great star of the 78 rpm, created marvels in the realms of both lieder and Italian opera. A renowned performer of Verdian roles, he sometimes recorded them in the original Italian, which was at that time rare for German singers.

[45] Another star of German song, Frida Leider (1888–1975) is shown here in one of the great Wagnerian roles, that of Brünnhilde in *Die Walküre*. The heavy headdress was at that time a prerequisite.

[46] The famous composer and conductor Richard Strauss (1864–1949), photographed with the soprano Lotte Lehmann (1888–1976) at a performance of Beethoven's opera *Fidelio* in 1927. Strauss wrote for her and often conducted her, but they never recorded together for Deutsche Grammophon.

[47] This 1925 advertisment brought together the greatest German conductors and composers of the time . . . not without a small error in Strauss's name.

[45]

[46]

[48]

[49]

[48] A publicity leaflet published by Deutsche Grammophon in 1926 that distinguishes records made for the internal German market (on the *Die Stimme seines Herrn* label) from those destined for export (on the Polydor label, created for this purpose in 1924).

[49] It was in 1924 that Deutsche Grammophon was authorized to reinstate the trademark *Die Stimme seines Herrn*, bringing to an end the ban that had been issued in 1918 at the end of World War I. It also became the title of a monthly magazine: the Gothic typography betrays a rediscovered German pride.

[50] Taken in 1931 in Berlin, this photograph is a reminder that labels' colors corresponded to price categories: brown (Braunetikett) was used for mid-priced records.

[50]

[51]...[53] In 1924 in Berlin, the German conductor Oskar Fried (1871–1941) recorded Mozart's *Eine kleine Nachtmusik* and the first-ever version of Mahler's *Resurrection* Symphony. The latter was considered a dual feat for the era because of the length of the work and the fact that it requires a huge orchestra.

[51]

[52]

[53]

[54]

[54] [55] In 1927 Richard Strauss recorded symphonic extracts of his opera *Intermezzo*, premiered three years earlier in Dresden, with Fritz Busch at the podium. The frightening Polydor character on the label is strongly reminiscent of German cinematic Expressionism, which began with Fritz Lang's *Metropolis* and Paul Wegener's *The Golem*.

[55]

Polyphon-Fabriken in Leipzig-Wahren

[56] Details (artists, factory, offices, and logo) from a Deutsche Grammophon publicity brochure dating from 1926.

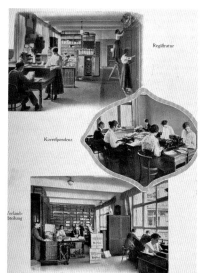

Grammophon-Fabriken in Hannover

[56]

In 1919 Deutsche Grammophon established the Polyphon-Sprechmaschinen und Schallplatten GmbH in Vienna; other subsidiary companies immediately followed, notably in Denmark and Sweden, and then—a case of poetic justice—in England (The Gramophone Ltd., 1926). In 1921 Joseph Berliner retired from the board of directors, and in 1922, from the supervisory board of the company: he had been the last of the original founders to remain actively involved in the company. The process of matrix production, known as "father–mother–son," was introduced the same year.

The first German radio broadcast took place in 1923; exchanges with this new medium rapidly became a source of fruitful collaboration. Bruno Walter and Otto Klemperer joined the label in 1924, with recordings of, respectively, Beethoven's *Coriolan* Overture with the Berlin Philharmonic and Beethoven's Symphony no. 1 with the Berlin Staatskapelle. In the same year, the arbitral tribunal set up under the Treaty of Versailles granted Deutsche Grammophon the authorization to reinstate the *Die Stimme seines Herrn* trademark, but only in German markets. The Polydor label was therefore created for export markets, and it was under this name that records produced by the company were distributed in Europe until 1949. As proof of the label's ambition, by the end of the era of acoustic recording, its catalogue included symphonies as imposing as Bruckner's Seventh and Mahler's Second (conducted by Fried), as well as all of Beethoven's symphonies, interpreted by various conductors. But Deutsche Grammophon was on the eve of a major revolution: the introduction of electrical recording, which would lend a new dimension to recorded sound from 1925 onward.

THE ERA OF ELECTRICAL RECORDING

Recalling the colorful era of acoustic recording, photographs show a handful of musicians clustered around the conductor, as close as possible to the recording apparatus. In spite of the progress that had been made, it was the musicians who suffered most from the technical limitations imposed by acoustic recording methods. In order to obtain the desired richness of sound, it was sometimes necessary to resort to crude hybrids, such as the "Stroh violin"—a violin with a horn in place of the normal body—or even to substitute one instrument with another. There was no doubt that electrical recording reproduced sound far more faithfully. From then on, mechanical transmission of vibrations to a cutting stylus gave way to a microphone and amplifier. It was perhaps this improvement in quality that convinced Wilhelm Furtwängler, who succeeded Arthur Nikisch as conductor of both the Berlin Philharmonic and the Leipzig Gewandhaus Orchestra, to sign his first record contracts in 1926, despite his scepticism. He chose to record the overture to Weber's *Der Freischütz* and Beethoven's Symphony no. 5, the latter often an introduction to conductors joining the label—Furtwängler recorded it as such, after Nikisch and before Karl Böhm, Carlos Kleiber, Christian Thielemann, and Gustavo Dudamel. He rerecorded this symphony several times between 1929 and 1937. Strauss, who was Furtwängler's elder by more than twenty years, also understood the benefit of rerecording major works: in the space of a couple of months in 1927 and 1928, he twice recorded Mozart's Symphony no. 40, the first time using the "Lichtstrahl" recording system developed by Brunswick, the second using a Western Electric system, which produced a much superior sound. In both cases, he chose the earlier version of the work without clarinets. Having also signed up Erich Kleiber, the Viennese music director of the Berlin State Opera, Deutsche Grammophon was able to offer its customers works by all of Berlin's prominent conductors. Less than ten years after the introduction of the new recording technique, all Beethoven's symphonies had been rerecorded.

[57]

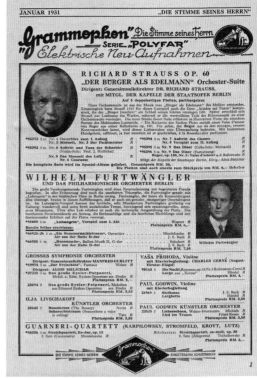

[58]

[59]

[60]

[57] A typical scene at a recording session at the time of acoustic recording: the famous Stroh violins, with horns in place of the normal bodies, clearly visible (1908). The conductor is Seidler-Winkler, and the tenor, positioned at the front of the stage, is Carl (or Karl) Jörn. Many decades later, the composer Mauricio Kagel facetiously highlighted the "indisputable" resemblance of Seidler-Winkler to Groucho Marx.

[58] Richard Strauss and Wilhelm Furtwängler (1886–1954) are given pride of place in this advertisement from 1931, which boasts of "new electrical recordings." But other important names from Deutsche Grammophon's catalogue are also mentioned: the Austrian conductor Alois Melichar and Czech violinist Váša Příhoda.

[59] The record label for Beethoven's Symphony no. 5 conducted by the German maestro Wilhelm Furtwängler (1886–1954) — his first recording of the work — which was released on the Brunswick label in 1928. Deutsche Grammophon had struck a reciprocal distribution deal with the American firm.

[60] This famous photograph was taken in Berlin on May 22, 1929 at a reception organized in honor of Arturo Toscanini and La Scala of Milan, that year's guests at the Berlin Festival. From left to right: Bruno Walter (1876–1962), Arturo Toscanini (1867–1957), Erich Kleiber (1890–1956), Otto Klemperer (1885–1973), and Wilhelm Furtwängler.

This period also witnessed the growth of the label, with renewed commercial vigor: in 1927 it signed a contract with the US record company Brunswick (each company agreed to distribute the recordings of the other); in the same year it released onto the market the Polyfar, the first record player with an electric loudspeaker. (The first recording made with this technology was released in 1928.) It also created subsidiary companies in Japan (Nippon Polydor Chikuochi K.K., 1928) and France (Société phonographique française Polydor S.A., 1929). Also in 1928 the respected Berlin choirmaster Bruno Kittel recorded Beethoven's *Missa Solemnis*, conducting his own choir and the Berlin Philharmonic—on eleven double-sided 78s! This recording of a reputedly difficult and austere work, which Kittel had successfully performed several times in 1927 in commemoration of the 100th anniversary of Beethoven's death, was new proof of Deutsche Grammophon's artistic ambitions and responsiveness, and it had a worldwide distribution. Popular repertoire, which was more likely to be reviewed, was not neglected, however: in the same year (1928), the Christmas song *Erzengel Gabriel verkündet den Hirten Christi Geburt* ("the Archangel Gabriel announcing the birth of Christ to the shepherds") was the first record ever to sell more than 1,000,000 copies in Germany. Deutsche Grammophon was thriving: there was an exponential growth in production; a rapid increase in the number of employees to several hundred; 5,500,000 records cut in 1928, and nearly 10,000,000 the following year, reaching a peak level of production of 83,000 records a day. Many singers attached to great opera houses, including tenors Helge Roswaenge, Koloman von Pataky, and Julius Patzak, negotiated contracts that allowed them to record in Berlin, which had become the recording capital of Germany.

THE DARK YEARS

But 1929, the year of Emile Berliner's death (his brother Joseph had died the previous year), was also the year of the Great Crash that, beginning in the United States, caused worldwide havoc. Aside from its devastating economic effects—mass unemployment, galloping inflation, and the collapse of the mark—the resultant brutal recession caused profound political upheaval. It led to the disintegration of the Weimar Republic, and, in January 1933, to the fateful rise to power of Hitler and the Nazis and the fateful consequences that ensued. Earlier, in 1930, Deutsche Grammophon's French subsidiary, directed by Erna Elchlepp, had recorded *Boléro*, under the direction of the work's composer Maurice Ravel, with the Orchestre Lamoureux—an historic recording, even though Ravel was less accomplished as a conductor than Strauss, or even Pfitzner. The conductor Alois Melichar was at that time the label's musical consultant, and he regularly recorded. From 1932 to 1936, Deutsche Grammophon saw its production fall to 2,500,000, then to 1,400,000 records, a figure low enough to jeopardize the company's future. Polyphon-Musikwerke and Deutsche Grammophon merged in 1932, and the Leipzig factory closed, but the corporate name remained. In 1937 Deutsche Grammophon AG was forced into liquidation; financed by the Deutsche Bank and radio company Telefunken (Telefunken Gesellschaft für drahtlose Telegraphie mbH), Deutsche Grammophon GmbH stayed in business.

These changes suggested the need to regain control, at least economically, in order to secure a publisher for a recording catalogue that included the top German artists (indeed, production figures climbed back up to 4,100,000 in 1938). The company's strategy until 1945 demonstrated both advance and withdrawal: on the one hand, there was innovation and a receptiveness to new ideas, while on the other, whether willingly or not, it battened down the hatches.

Innovation was evident in 1934 with the arrival of the concept of high fidelity (hi-fi), which extended the band of recorded frequencies from 30 to 8,000 Hz, thus improving sound quality still further. In 1931, in the United States, the Bell Telephone Company undertook its first stereophonic testing with Leopold Stokowski; "Raumton," the "spatial sound" devised by German engineers, had foreshadowed it. Meanwhile, Deutsche Grammophon seized every opportunity to sign new artists. One was a certain Herbert von Karajan, the young Kapellmeister of the Berlin State Opera, who recorded Mozart's overture to *The Magic Flute* in 1938, although his contract was not signed until 1939, the year in which Europe was plunged into World War II. Also noteworthy from this period are the great Italian conductor Victor de Sabata, whose activities in Nazi Germany provoked the wrath of well-known antifascist Arturo Toscanini, and the Dutch conductor of the Dresden Philharmonic, Paul van Kempen, as well as Bach apostles Karl Straube and Günther Ramin. Other artists signed by the company at this time included such German leading lights as singers Erna Berger, Tiana Lemnitz, Walther Ludwig, Franz Völker, and Viorica Ursuleac and pianist Elly Ney. In 1938 the company introduced the *Meisterklasse* series, which sometimes reproduced a photograph of the artist on the record label.

The company's retreat was, evidently, in direct correlation with the villainous anti-Semitic policies of the Nazis, who brutally blacklisted great Jewish artists who had been valuable assets for Deutsche Grammophon, including Walter, Klemperer, and the violinist Bronislaw Huberman, all of whom were forced into exile. Their records disappeared from a catalogue that subsequently became colonized by recordings of marches and Nazi songs, a crude and immediately apparent sign of the influence exerted by the regime. Like so many other services, institutions, and companies, Deutsche Grammophon became an instrument in the service of Nazi propaganda. The regime also subtly reorganized industries: in 1941, following an agreement between Siemens and AEG, both of which prospered under the new regime, AEG inherited Telefunken Gesellschaft's shares, while Siemens acquired those of Deutsche Grammophon, which was then integrated into the latter's electroacoustic division.

"Aryan" artists went from one world to another as if nothing had happened, at least so it appeared: Bruno Kittel cut a record in 1942, the "first integrated recording" of Bach's *St. Matthew Passion*, once again uniting his choir with the Berlin Philharmonic. Despite the fact that eighteen movements were left out, the recording still took up eighteen double-sided 78s. The demand by the Japanese subsidiary for this recording led to the matrices being transported there by submarine. Kittel had also recorded, the previous year, Mozart's *Requiem*, with a rewritten libretto from which all allusions to the Jewish roots of Christianity had been removed. The threatening letter that the Gestapo sent to Deutsche Grammophon as late as May 9, 1942, in which it ordered the company to stop manufacturing matrices of recordings by Jewish artists, was another ominous sign of things to come. (The previous year, in Munich, Richard Strauss had recorded his symphonic poem *Ein Heldenleben*.) The predicted end was near: raw goods were rationed; the number of titles featured in the catalogue, as well as the number of new recordings, had been dictatorially reduced; and the Hanover factory was damaged by Allied bombing in 1943. The offices and recording studios in Berlin were destroyed in 1944 and 1945. Thus ended, and not just symbolically, one of the darkest periods of Deutsche Grammophon's history.

[61]

[62]

[61] Emile Berliner, the founding father of Deutsche Grammophon was awarded the prestigious Franklin Medal in April 1929 in recognition of his pioneering work in the field of recording and sound. He died shortly afterward, in August of the same year.

[62]…[64] During the dark years of mass unemployment, the normally colorful Polydor labels were printed in black to cut printing costs. The French label (63) is for a recording of Ravel's *Boléro*, conducted by the composer himself (64) in 1930.

[63]

[64]

[65]

[65] Hitler and the Nazis came to power in January 1933. The partisan infiltration brutally affected all trades, Deutsche Grammophon included. Note the sinister swastika, and, in the front row, uniformed storm troopers, no doubt coming from among the firm's personnel.

[66] An unforgettable Queen of the Night from Mozart's *The Magic Flute*: the coloratura soprano Erna Berger (1900–1990) was one of the stars of German song during the dark years from 1933 to 1945.

[67] During these years Deutsche Grammophon engaged a brilliant and ambitious young conductor: His name was Herbert von Karajan (1908–1989). Here he is seen on an advertisement promoting one of his recordings, released in the *Meisterklasse* collection.

[66]

[67]

[68]

[69]

[70]

[68] The Hanover factory in 1943, after the Allied bombings.

[69] A rare photograph of the German conductor Bruno Kittel (1870–1948), here with Wilhelm Furtwängler.

[70] Reproduction of a formal notice sent by the Gestapo in Berlin to Deutsche Grammophon on May 9, 1942. "The records and matrices in your possession of recordings made with Jewish artists will be confiscated in accordance with article. . . . From now on, the production of new records or matrices from these recordings of Jewish artists is forbidden. Infringement of this decree will result in severe action being taken by the Secret State Police (Gestapo)."

ELISABETH KOEHLER

Elisabeth Koehler joined Polydor France in 1957, working for the popular music division before joining the Deutsche Grammophon division at the beginning of the 1960s as press officer, a position that she held until 1991. It was a demanding job that allowed her to establish close working relationships based on trust with a number of artists. Here she recalls some of her many memories.

I wanted to call a press conference for the release of the *Complete Beethoven Symphonies* (1962–1963), conducted by Herbert von Karajan. We had received the records, the boxes, and the leaflets separately and needed to package them. Sviatoslav Richter was visiting Paris at the time, and (I don't know what came over me) I suggested to my boss, M. Raymond Ducarre, that we ask him to be the "honorary packer." Having got the go-ahead from my boss—though he was somewhat surprised—I made my suggestion to Richter. He accepted immediately, saying: "I love Karajan, I admire him enormously, but I'm not good at gift wrapping, so I'll need to arrive an hour before everyone else so I can practice getting it right." And so, as arranged, he arrived with us, donned his overalls, and got to work. That was how our press conference happened, very informally, as always!

Just before the end-of-year festivities the following year, a journalist friend telephoned me and asked me if we had any special launches planned for the occasion. I don't know why, but I replied, "We're exhausted! Last year was relatively easy with the release of the *Complete Beethoven Symphonies*, but this year, we've had a lot more work. So much, in fact, that we've sent a petition round requesting that they send us to a beauty parlor for Christmas." Of course, it was just a joke, but my friend replied, "Send me the petition. We'll publish it!" So, following this conversation, we wrote one. My boss, who I asked to sign it, gave me a talking-to at first: "What? An in-house petition? We've never done that before!" But, of course, once I had explained to him that it was a publicity stunt, he agreed. I then phoned a friend who worked in a beauty parlor, and she came to our premises with her colleagues. One of the offices had been specially converted into a beauty parlor, and we organized our end-of-year press conference there!

Herbert von Karajan gave very few interviews. The first one he agreed to during the time that I was press officer was in relation to Brahms's symphonies. It was in 1964. Our director had gone to Berlin earlier to prepare for the interview with the great journalist Micheline Banzet. Karajan's private secretary, Andre von Mattoni, received them, adding, "The master will give you three minutes." When Micheline Banzet met the maestro, she greeted him but told him that she was going to catch her plane because three minutes was quite simply impossible. Karajan replied, "We'll make time tomorrow morning." He gave her a long interview, illustrating some of his replies at the piano. It was marvelous. Over the years, I managed to persuade him to grant many other interviews. He trusted me. I owe a lot to Mme von Karajan, who often supported my efforts in this respect.

Whenever Leonard Bernstein came to Paris, I would pick him up at the airport and drive him to the Crillon, where he had a magnificent suite on the fifth floor with an unobstructed view over Paris, which he loved. One Sunday afternoon in 1981, he had just given a concert at the Théâtre des Champs-Elysées and was due to leave the following day for the United States, where he was to perform the same program. After the concert, a man climbed onto the stage and grabbed the score that the conductor had annotated. The stage manager had let him do so, thinking that he was Bernstein's secretary. But he was a thief! We released urgent statements in the hope of finding the score and contacted the police because we'd been sent a demand for money in exchange for its safe return. I think that the blackmailer got scared, because following the second radio announcement that we released, the radio station France Musique received an anonymous phone call telling them where the score had been left. Philippe Caloni, one of their great broadcasters at that time, and I rushed to retrieve it, and just had time to return it to Bernstein, who was already at the airport and about to catch his flight. He was so happy that he knelt down and kissed Philippe Caloni's knees, and when I returned home, I found an enormous bouquet of flowers that he had had sent before he left.

The first time that Gundula Janowitz came to Paris, she was completely unknown here. We knew only that she had collaborated on the *Complete Beethoven* that Karajan had conducted, but we didn't yet know her. She was replacing Irmgard Seefried, who was ill, at the eleventh hour, in a very important televised concert. We needed to make a press announcement to this effect, and her name seemed to be so difficult to remember that we had to repeat it, and do the same when she appeared on stage. She arrived on the day of the concert. It was November, the weather was appalling, and her flight was delayed. In fact, she was so late that when she eventually turned up at rehearsal, the musicians had already left. She had to rehearse with just a pianist. Despite these difficulties, she gave a tremendous performance. She charmed everyone. That evening, we dined with her and told her how much everyone had admired her interpretation of Agatha's aria from *der Freischütz*. She replied, somewhat embarrassed, that she had learned it only that morning, on the plane . . .

1945–1979

RÉMY LOUIS

The deep wounds inflicted by twelve years of murderous madness left the world battered and Germany shattered; by the middle of May 1945, the great musical centers were in ruins. However, just as orchestras and operas somehow or other managed to reopen their doors several weeks later, so, too, what remained of the Podbielskistrasse factory was opened and its employees returned to work; a modest production line was also started up in Berlin, with the authorization of the Anglo-American military command. The license to manufacture records was once again granted in August 1946.

A retrospective view made it clear that Deutsche Grammophon needed to look for new ways forward, to find new perspectives. The concept of Archiv Produktion, laid out in 1946, and its inception in 1947 was a visible outworking of this decision: in the minds of Ernst von Siemens, Siegfried Janzen, Hans Domizlaff, Helmut Haertel, and Fred Hamel (the first producer of the new label), it meant promoting early music, resurrecting forgotten repertoires—from the Renaissance to the Baroque—and entrusting them to musicians who could interpret the original sources and consider stylistic issues. To that purpose, Hamel proposed setting up a research institute with "theory-based" and "practical" departments, the latter commanding a chamber choir, an instrumental ensemble, and its own recording studio. In an ironic twist of fate, banished musician Otto Klemperer had promoted a return to the use of early instruments for playing Bach in the late 1920s, while the Mozart Festival held in Vienna in 1941, under the aegis of the Third Reich, also included a concert given on these same instruments. The first Archiv record was cut in 1947 by blind organist Helmut Walcha: Bach's Toccata and Fugue in D Minor, played on the organ of St. Jacob in Lübeck. For thirty years, Walcha remained associated with the label. Edith Picht-Axenfeld, Gustav Scheck, and Fritz Lehmann soon joined him.

[02]

[03]

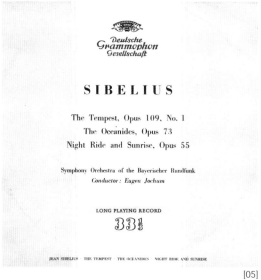
[04]

[06]

[05]

[01] Original sketches (pencil on tracing paper) of the "stylized tulips," designed by Hans Domizlaff (1892–1971), that characterized Deutsche Grammophon's covers from the late 1940s onward.

[02] Dr. Fred Hamel, the first director of the Archiv Produktion label, created in 1946 to explore early and Baroque music.

[03] Wolfgang Siegling, seen here in 1950, was a true publicity and marketing guru at Deutsche Grammophon for more than twenty years.

[04] Starting in 1948, each label had its own visual identity according to a specific type of recorded music. Yellow (Deutsche Grammophon) was used for regular classical music, red (Polydor) for easy listening and variety, and silver (Archiv Produktion) for early music.

[05] The first 33 rpm microgroove records left the Hanover factory in 1951. The yellow central band was a distinctive feature on record sleeves of that time.

[06] Blind from the age of sixteen, the German organist Helmut Walcha (1907–1991) was a central figure in Archiv Produktion's catalogue. He was responsible for two major and complete recordings of J. S. Bach's organ works: one in mono, the other in stereo.

THE YELLOW LABEL

Deutsche Grammophon's objective was also to return to normal without losing its technical expertise, in as much as shortages would allow. The 78 rpm record was living on borrowed time. From 1946 Deutsche Grammophon systematized the first use of recording on magnetic tape, making use of pioneering research that had been carried out by German engineers during World War II. Turnover took an upward trend: 1,650,000 marks in 1947 and 1,800,000 records in 1948. The first post-war catalogue came out in the year of the company's 50th anniversary, which was also that of the monetary reform and the Berlin Blockade—wisely, production was moved back to a single site in Hanover. Domizlaff, a graphic designer and marketing consultant who had come from Siemens, advocated that each segment of Deutsche Grammophon's repertoire should be matched to a different type of product and given its own visual identity: easy listening for Polydor (red), early music for Archiv (silver), and "traditional" classical music for Deutsche Grammophon (yellow). The idea became standard practice; the Yellow Label, with its crown of stylized tulips, was born in 1949; meanwhile, the *Die Stimme seines Herrn* trademark was made over to Electrola, the German branch of EMI. In a refinement that betrayed the changing times, the calligraphy used for the trademark was the same as that of the company logo. The layout of the tulips around the edge of the label was designed to create a stroboscopic effect, appearing stationary when the rotational speed of the record turntable was correctly adjusted.

The invention of the variable-groove record in 1949 doubled the playing time of 78s to nine minutes per side. New talent was sought with renewed energy—many artists who had been active in Germany after 1933 had to leave before denazification commissions in 1946 and 1947. Among those signed were the conductor Eugen Jochum and French pianist Monique Haas. Another important figure was the Hungarian Ferenc Fricsay, who was discovered in Salzburg in 1947, engaged the following year at the Deutsche Opera Berlin, and named principal conductor of the RIAS Symphonie-Orchester, the radio orchestra founded by the US occupying authorities (RIAS—the name used until 1956—was an acronym for "Broadcasting in the American Sector"). He represented a real revival, as much for his liberal repertoire as for his precise and alert style, a characteristic common among Central European musicians. His first recording was of Tchaikovsky's Symphony no. 5 with the Berlin Philharmonic in 1949. The young baritone Dietrich Fischer-Dieskau also took his first steps with the Yellow Label in 1949, recording an extract from Puccini's *La Bohème* and Brahms's *Four Serious Songs* in 1949 and opening the way to an unparalleled collaboration. But another technical revolution was under way: the introduction of the microgroove record, invented in the United States the previous decade. Deutsche Grammophon commissioned the services of Wolfgang Siegling, who had also come from Siemens. For twenty-five years, he planned the performance, sales, and marketing strategies, defining the company's identity. Hans-Werner Steinhausen joined the ranks as technical director (later becoming vice president): he became the custodian of the Yellow Label's reputation for technical and artistic excellence. And, indeed, this was the beginning of a golden age, when Deutsche Grammophon decided to dedicate itself just to "classical music" (that is, early and Baroque, classical and Romantic, modern and contemporary): the full identification of the trademark with the goods it promoted—"Deutsche Grammophon is Classical Music"—was the result of a genuine artistic philosophy.

[07]

[08]

[09]

[10]

[07] Eugen Jochum was a remarkable interpreter of the works of Carl Orff. His legacy includes benchmark recordings of the *Trionfi*, the trilogy of cantatas that includes *Carmina Burana, Catulla Carmina*, and *Triompho di Aphrodite*. Only the series recorded in mono is complete.

[08] LPM 18 303, recorded in 1952 at the Amerika Haus theater in Munich.

[09] Two Bavarians at work: the conductor Eugen Jochum (1902–1987) and the composer Carl Orff (1895–1982), seen here in 1967 during the recording of *Carmina Burana*, which has become a great classic of the Deutsche Grammophon catalogue.

[10] SLPM 138 831, recorded in Berlin in 1962. A pupil of Rudolf Serkin and Robert Casadesus, the French pianist Monique Haas (1909–1987) was considered one of the best performers of the music of her compatriots Debussy and Ravel.

[11]

[12]

[13]

[14]

[15]

[16]

[11]…[16] The quintessential lieder singer, Dietrich Fischer-Dieskau (born in 1925) was also an outstanding opera singer, here seen in his debut role as the Marquis of Posa in Verdi's *Don Carlos* [16] in Berlin in 1948 and as Mandryka, the lead male role in Richard Strauss's *Arabella*. The perfect partnership he formed with the Swiss soprano Lisa della Casa (born in 1918), nicknamed "Arabellissima," gave rise to beautiful evenings [13] at the National Theatre of Munich over many seasons.

[17]

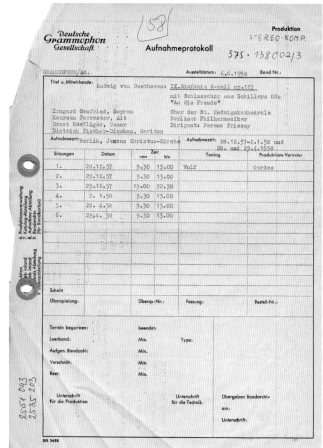

[18]

[17] Berlin 1961: the Hungarian conductor Ferenc Fricsay (1914–1963) rehearsing with the Radio-Symphonie-Orchester Berlin (RSO) and the violinist Yehudi Menuhin (1916–1999). The two musicians were united by a deep friendship. Menuhin even once waived his fee to help pay for new suits for the musicians of the former RIAS-Symphonie-Orchester!

[18] A production schedule from June 6, 1958, detailing the recording sessions for Beethoven's Symphony no. 9 with a selection of the label's most prominent soloists: soprano Irmgard Seefried, contralto Maureen Forrester, tenor Ernst Haefliger, and leading baritone Dietrich Fischer-Dieskau.

[19] The booklet that accompanied the red boxed set of Beethoven's Symphony no. 9, recorded by Fricsay in 1958 (SLPM 138 002), which was a jewel of the catalogue in the 1950s.

[20] LPM 1855/6, recorded in Berlin in 1953.

[21] Ferenc Fricsay in Berlin in 1954 during a rehearsal with the RIAS-Symphonie-Orchester, of which he was the principal conductor. He had been offered this position by Elsa Schiller, who was responsible for the classical music division of the RIAS before becoming artistic director of Deutsche Grammophon in 1952. Fricsay's numerous recordings occupied a central place in the catalogue during the 1950s.

[19]

[20]

[21]

[22]

[23]

Dr. Hans-Werner Steinhausen
Deutsche Grammophon Gesellschaft, 60 Jahre alt

Dr.-Ing. Hans-Werner Steinhausen, Geschäftsführer der Deutschen Grammophon Gesellschaft und Vorstandsmitglied der Philips Phonographische Industrie N. V. (PPI), Baarn Holland, vollendet am 22. Juni 1966 das 60. Lebensjahr.

Der Gedanke, Muse und Technik miteinander gleichsam versöhnt zu sehen, begleitete Steinhausen schon in sehr frühen Jahren. Musik war für Steinhausen, der 1906 in Berlin-Spandau geboren wurde, bereits im Elternhaus ein primäres Erlebnis. Die Mutter, Schülerin von Humperdinck, war Pianistin. Und der Sohn trug sich damals mit dem Gedanken, ausübender Musiker zu werden. Die Beschäftigung mit der Schallplatte, zunächst als Hobby, war es nicht zuletzt, die dann jedoch das Interesse an elektro-akustischen Dingen überwiegen ließ.

Nach dem Abschluß des Humanistischen Gymnasiums bezog Steinhausen die Technische Hochschule Berlin, die er 1930 als Diplomingenieur verließ. Zunächst wirkte er einige Zeit als Patentingenieur in der „Fernsprechanlage-Baugesellschaft", kehrt aber dann — ebenfalls für einige Jahre — wieder an die Technische Hochschule zurück. 1935 erwarb er den Titel des Dr.-Ing. und trat als Entwicklungsingenieur bei Telefunken ein. Hier beschäftigte er sich vor allem mit der Verbesserung der Wiedergabequalität von Rundfunkgeräten. In diesen Jahren begegnete er auch Hugo Wünsch, Direktor der Deutschen Grammophon Gesellschaft, die damals zum Telefunken-Konzern gehörte.

Nach dem Kriege ging Steinhausen als technischer Leiter zur Telefunkenplatte nach Hannover. 1950 trat Steinhausen als Leiter der gesamten Entwicklung bei der Deutschen Grammophon Gesellschaft in Hannover ein, deren Nachkriegsgeschichte er auf seinem ureigenen Gebiete bis zum heutigen Tage mitbestimmt hat. 1953 Prokurist, 1957 Fabrikdirektor, 1958 Ordentlicher Geschäftsführer und 1965 Vorstandsmitglied der PPI — Stationen und Bestätigungen eines Werdeganges, dessen wichtigste Ereignisse die Langspielplatte und die Stereophonie waren.

[24]

[22] … [25] Dr. Hans-Werner Steinhausen joined Deutsche Grammophon in 1950 as technical director. It was he (with acoustician Heinrich Keilholz) who defined the very strict rules governing record production. For example, one side of a 33 rpm record was never allowed to exceed twenty-eight minutes—this was the only way to ensure that the grooves were sufficiently wide to allow reproduction of a broad dynamic range. Some record companies did not hesitate to record two Beethoven symphonies on the same record, but this led to not only reduction in dynamic range but also problems with the needle jumping because of the narrowness of the grooves. Deutsche Grammophon would never have tolerated such things. Quality came at a price, however: a record from the Hanover factory cost around 24 marks at a time when the average monthly salary was 350 marks.

[25]

[26] Wilhelm Kempff (1895–1991) in communion with Beethoven or Brahms. A pianist, but above all a poet, he brought an evocative and distinctive mood to everything he played.

[27] LPM 18 376, recorded in Dresden in 1957.

[28] LPM 18 371, recorded in 1953 at the Jesus-Christus-Kirche in Berlin.

JOHANNES BRAHMS
Konzert für Klavier und Orchester Nr.1
d-moll op.15

A-Seite: Maestoso   B-Seite: Adagio · Rondo: Allegro non troppo

Concerto for Piano and Orchestra No.1 in D minor, Op.15 · Concerto pour piano et orchestre nº1 en ré mineur op.15

Wilhelm Kempff, Piano
Sächsische Staatskapelle Dresden · Dirigent: Franz Konwitschny

LPM 18 376   HI-FI

LUDWIG VAN BEETHOVEN
Fünf Klavierkonzerte
THE FIVE CONCERTOS
FOR PIANO
AND ORCHESTRA

WILHELM KEMPFF
BERLINER PHILHARMONIKER
PAUL VAN KEMPEN

WIGMORE HALL

WIGMORE STREET, W.I

THE

AMADEUS

STRING QUARTET

NORBERT BRAININ *(Violin)*   **PETER SCHIDLOF** *(Viola)*

SIEGMUND NISSEL *(Violin)*   **MARTIN LOVETT** *('Cello)*

SATURDAY AFTERNOON

JANUARY 10th, 1948

at 3 p.m.

TICKETS (including Tax): Reserved 9/- and 6/-; Unreserved 3/-

(All bookable in advance)

May be obtained from BOX OFFICE, WIGMORE HALL (WEL. 2141), usual Ticket Offices and

IBBS & TILLETT LTD., 124, Wigmore Street, W.I

Telephone: Welbeck 2325 (3 lines)   Hours: 10—5. Saturdays, 10—12

Telegrams: "Organol, Wesdo, London."   Ticket Office: Welbeck 8418

Vail & Co., Ltd., E.C. (1947)   For Programme P.T.O.

[29]

[30]

[31]

Deutsche
Grammophon
Gesellschaft

Robert Schumann

ROBERT SCHUMANN

Sinfonie Nr. 4
d-moll op. 120

Berliner Philharmoniker
Dirigent: Wilhelm Furtwängler

LANGSPIELPLATTE
33

ROBERT SCHUMANN · SINFONIE Nr. 4 d-moll op. 120   16063 LP

[32]

[33]

[31]…[33] Wilhelm Furtwängler made few studio recordings for Deutsche Grammophon after the Second World War. Schumann's Symphony no. 4, recorded in 1953, is one of these legendary recordings (16063 LP). Deutsche Grammophon also knew how to make the most of the many concert recordings that had been preserved by radio stations, from which came this version of Beethoven's Symphony no. 5, recorded live in Berlin in 1947 (LPM 18 724).

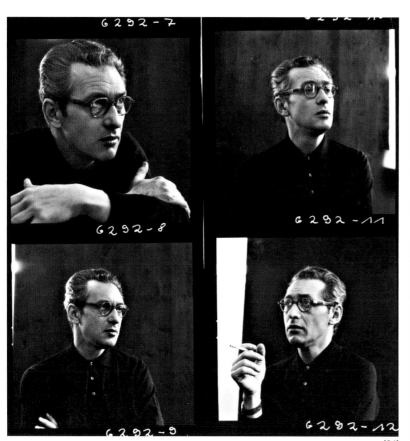

[34]

[35]

[36]

[37]

[38]

[34] … [37] These three albums (SLPM 138 868, 138 111, and 138 084) were recorded between 1959 and 1963 at the Jesus-Christus-Kirche in Berlin, a former church that was transformed into a recording studio. One of the best-loved pianists of the 1950s and '60s, the Hungarian Géza Anda (1921–1976) was particularly noted for his major recordings of Mozart, Chopin, and Schumann.

[38] Harpsichordist, organist, choirmaster, and conductor Karl Richter (1926–1981) was a true cantor in the German tradition. From 1953 he made his mark with Archiv's productions, in particular with his dense and powerful vision of Bach.

The first microgroove records left the Hanover factories in 1951. Made from polyvinyl chloride (PVC), they were supplied in two sizes: 25 cm (fifteen minutes per side) and 30 cm (thirty minutes per side). The rotational speed, 33⅓ rpm was the same for both sizes. The first ones were sold with a cardboard cover, inside which the record was protected in a machine-sewn sleeve—glue that would not damage the records had not yet been invented. Before the days of stereophonic sound, vinyl offered artists unforeseen possibilities: Wilhelm Kempff (who between 1951 and 1956 made the first recording for Deutsche Grammophon of all Beethoven's piano sonatas), the Amadeus Quartet (which, founded in 1947, epitomized the Yellow Label, following the example of Fricsay, Fischer-Dieskau, and Kempff), Wilhelm Furtwängler (who, though under contract with EMI, nevertheless entrusted Deutsche Grammophon with his imposing Symphony no. 2, as well as conducting works by Haydn, Schubert, and Schumann), Karl Böhm (Beethoven's Symphony no. 5, 1953) and Karl Richter (Schütz's *Musikalische Exequien*, Archiv, 1953) all joined Deutsche Grammophon. Others, such as Kempff and the great pianist Géza Anda (a magnificent interpreter of Schumann) returned to the company.

THE FIRST GOLDEN AGE

Deutsche Grammophon's artistic policy was epitomized by Elsa Schiller, a visionary producer—as were her contemporaries Walter Legge (EMI), John Culshaw (Decca), and John Pfeiffer (RCA) for their respective labels. For a woman to hold such a position (1952–1963) was at that time in itself remarkable; the fact that she had also, before the war, created a chamber orchestra that she conducted herself adds to her uniqueness—female conductors were then extremely rare, with the exception of the pioneering Antonia Brico. Schiller applied herself to rebuilding and developing the catalogue: whenever there was an important new technological innovation, part of the catalogue disappeared, or became obsolete. Her artistic achievements were spectacular: the first complete opera Deutsche Grammophon recorded after the war (Lortzing's *Zar und Zimmermann*, conducted by Ferdinand Leitner, 1952); the first unabridged play (Goethe's *Faust*, 1954, directed by Gustaf Gründgens, who also played the role of Mephistopheles—*Mephisto* was also the title of a novel by Klaus Mann, who grievously denounced the way in which his friend Gründgens had sold his soul to the Nazis); the introduction of stereo (Bach played by Walcha on the Alkmaar organ, 1956, Archiv); a series of Mozart operas entrusted to Fricsay (*The Abduction from the Seraglio*, *The Magic Flute*, *The Marriage of Figaro*, and *Don Giovanni*); Strauss operas conducted by Böhm, who was a close friend of the composer's (*Der Rosenkavalier* and *Elektra*, with the Dresden Staatskapelle and the Strauss orchestra par excellence)—so many exemplary recordings. Fritz Lehmann (engaged with both Deutsche Grammophon and Archiv before his premature death in 1956), Hans Rosbaud, Jochum (the complete symphonies of Beethoven recorded partly in mono in Munich and Berlin, which were later, unjustly, eclipsed by Karajan's sets, as well as benchmark recordings of Bruckner and Orff), Igor Markevitch, and Franz Konwitschny all cut significant records, whose virtues have recently been rediscovered. Recitals by singers, too, followed one after the other, notably those by Irmgard Seefried, Maria Stader, Rita Streich, and Astrid Varnay. Other important recordings included Monteverdi's *Orfeo* conducted by August Wenzinger (with tenor Helmut Krebs, 1955), Bach's *St. John Passion* (Ramin, 1954), and Bach's *The Art of the Fugue* (Walcha, 1956), all on the Archiv label, which had methodically organized musical research according to twelve music-historical "chapters" or fields of study.

[39]

[40]

[41]

[39] [40] The recording industry's history has been written by the few great producers who knew how to pick the right artist at the right time and, no less importantly, how to entrust them with the repertoires for which they were most suited. Elsa Schiller was definitely one such producer. As head of the label from 1952, she made the decision to record the first part of Goethe's *Faust* in 1954, a key work from a popular German poet and playwright. Reassured by the sales performance, which had required a large investment of 50,000 marks at the time, Deutsche Grammophon recorded the second part in 1959.

[41] A representative example of the quality of Archiv's productions. The heavy, fabric-covered boxed sets were a pleasure to touch, even before you listened to the music they contained.

[42]

[43]

[44]

[45]

[46]

[42]…[45] The studio recordings of Mozart's operas made by Fricsay in Berlin (1954–1960, two in Italian and two in German) were a landmark of the 1950s. They have lost none of their vigor or stylistic relevance. Here they are presented in their original editions.

[46] Fischer-Dieskau was one of Fricsay's favorite collaborators; here they are seen during rehearsals of Mozart's *Don Giovanni*, which was performed (in German) for the reopening of the Berlin Deutsche Oper in 1961. It was to be the last large-scale opera production conducted by the great maestro.

[47]

[48]

[47] Richard Strauss and Karl Böhm, seen here in 1935, were united by genuine affection and friendship. The composer dedicated his opera *Daphne* to the conductor: Böhm premiered it in 1938 in Dresden, and in 1964 recorded it live in Vienna for Deutsche Grammophon.

[48] Recorded at the Lukaskirche in Dresden in 1958, *Der Rosenkavalier* (SLPM 138 040/43) inaugurated a glorious series of opera recordings made in Dresden until 1979 by the Austrian conductor Karl Böhm (1894–1981) at the head of the magnificent Dresden Staatskapelle—the Strauss orchestra par excellence—of which he had been chief conductor from 1934 to 1942.

[49] Fritz Lehmann (1904–1956), who died prematurely, was unusual in being one of the rare musicians whose recordings were released, in the 1950s, on both Archiv and Deutsche Grammophon labels, for this renowned Bach specialist also recorded a large classical and Romantic repertoire.

[49]

[50]

[51]

[52]

[50] Opening up to other traditions: Igor Markevitch made recordings for Deutsche Grammophon from the early 1950s, both in Paris (with the Orchestre Lamoureux) and in Berlin (with the Berlin Philharmonic), often to the great benefit of French music.

[51] LPM 18 469, recorded in November 1957 at the Théâtre des Champs-Élysées in Paris.

[52] Unjustly forgotten until its recent reappearance in the *Original Masters* series, Jochum's complete Beethoven symphonies, recorded with two orchestras (partly in mono, partly in stereo) is a splendid testament to this conductor's art.

[53]

[54]

[55]

[56]

[57]

[58]

[59]

[60]

[61]

[53]…[61] A vocal anthology typical of the 1950s, this recording brings together three singers favoured by Elsa Schiller: Maria Stader, Irmgard Seefried, and Rita Streich sang in both Vienna and Berlin while also pursuing international careers.

During the mid-1950s, experimentation and the search for new territories were continuous. Launched in 1953, the 45 rpm polyethylene record, which had a diameter of 17 cm and a playing time of five minutes per side, was hugely successful in the area of pop music; the extended-play 45, something of a hybrid (with the same specifications but with eight minutes of playing time per side), was less successful. The record for children released in 1956 for the bicentenary of the birth of Mozart, *Wolfgang von Gott beliebt* ("Wolfgang loved by God"), is worthy of mention; not only did it remain in the catalogue for more than thirty years, but it also gave birth to an extensive lineage. Another spoken-word record of a different genre paid tribute to the Berlin Philharmonic on the occasion of its 75th anniversary in 1957; it was written and narrated by the noted critic Hans-Heinz Stuckenschmidt. Following in the footsteps of those founded before the war, new subsidiary companies were born: Polydor Ltd. (which became Polydor K.K.) in Japan (1953), Heliodor (which became Polydor Ltd.) in Great Britain (1954), and Polydor S.A. in France (1956). Market exploration in Eastern Europe enriched Deutsche Grammophon's catalogue with some outstanding figures, including Sviatoslav Richter, David Oistrakh, and Evgeny Mravinsky (conducting Tchaikovsky symphonies). Partnerships were launched from east to west, with Eterna in East Germany and with the North American branch of Decca in the United States (American Decca). Deutsche Grammophon's artistic and commercial success was considerable: with an annual production of 15,000,000 records, it manufactured half the records sold in the German market. In 1956 Archiv released Mozart's *Requiem* (conducted by Jochum) in a splendid fabric-lined presentation box; the work had been recorded the previous year in a public performance given as part of a full mass celebrated at St. Stephen's Cathedral in Vienna.

It was also in 1956 that Deutsche Grammophon moved its headquarters to Hamburg. The manufacturing base remained in Hanover; a new site was built at Hanover-Langenhagen to respond to demand (from 1959 it manufactured records using an injection molding process). On the eve of its 60th anniversary, the Yellow Label developed a new visual in the form of a cartouche (black type on a yellow background with a white inner border), created by graphic artist Gerhard Noack, who drew his inspiration for the design from a manual of embellishments published in 1888; the calligraphic Deutsche Grammophon Gesellschaft trademark was featured over three lines, with the tulip crown resting on top. The new visual, which first appeared in 1958, continues to be used, with only slight modifications. Another significant event was the release by Deutsche Grammophon, in partnership with the German Music Council (Deutscher Musikrat), of two boxed sets of records devoted to twenty-two contemporary composers of different generations and aesthetics. Their generic title, *Musica Nova*, echoed that of the famous concert series *Musica Viva*, which had been taking place in Munich since 1945, organized by composer Karl-Amadeus Hartmann. The chosen composers were also regularly featured by the very active contemporary music department of WDR (West German Broadcasting) in Cologne; in particular, a certain Karlheinz Stockhausen, who soon became a central figure in Deutsche Grammophon.

[62]

[63]

[64]

[65]

[62]…[65] The 45-rpm record found worldwide fame in song and popular music. But in the early 1950s, Deutsche Grammophon also used this format for small-scale classical works, such as overtures, short works, and short symphonies. The French edition of *Eine kleine Nachtmusik (Une petite musique de nuit)* shows Jochum recording the work with a small orchestra.

[66]

[67]

[68]

[69]

[66]…[69] The conductor Evgeny Mravinsky (1903–1988) and David Oistrakh (1908–1974) playing chess with the latter's son Igor, himself a remarkable violinist. Deutsche Grammophon prided itself on making these two great artists from the Eastern bloc known in the West.

[70]

[71]

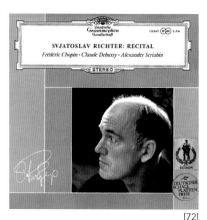

[72]

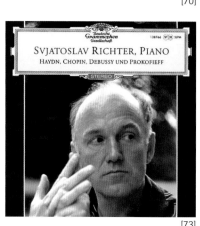

[73]

[70] Sviatoslav Richter's late appearance in the West was explosive (an effect that his colleague Emil Gilels, himself a great artist, had predicted). Richter (1915–1997) made few recordings with Deutsche Grammophon, but all of them are significant. Tchaikovsky's Piano Concerto no. 1 with Karajan remains one of the most controversial.

[71] SLPM 138 822, recorded in 1962 in the Golden Hall of the Musikverein in Vienna.

[72] SLPM 138 849, recorded live in 1962 during a concert tour of Italy.

[73] SLPM 138 766, recorded in 1961 at Wembley Town Hall in London.

[74]

[75]

[76]

[77]

[74]…[77] Very different in style and aesthetics, Karl Amadeus Hartmann (1905–1963) and Karlheinz Stockhausen (1928–2007) were two major German composers of the twentieth century. Both naturally found their place in the *Musica Nova* series launched by Deutsche Grammophon in the mid-1950s to bear witness to the vitality of postwar contemporary music.

[78] Promotional materials published (circa 1960) to explain the transition to stereo. Many of the records bearing the red "Stereo" label are much sought after by collectors because of their high quality.

[79] In the 1960s, publications announcing new releases were painstakingly produced and highly illustrated, as can be seen in these four pages from a French catalogue; reminiscent of present-day celebrity magazines, they were introducing true stars…

„Stereo" und „compatible" – zwei neue Begriffe im Reiche der Schallplatte. Über ihre Auswirkung und Bedeutung wollen wir Ihnen hier berichten.

WAS IST STEREOPHONIE

DIE NEUE TON-AUFZEICHNUNG

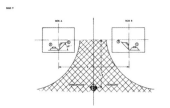

STEREO-MUSIKGLOCKE

[78]

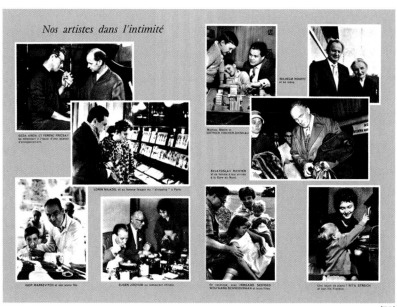

Nos artistes dans l'intimité

[79]

[80]

[81]

[82]

[83]

[80]…[82] According to the American musicologist and harpsichordist Ralph Kirkpatrick (1911–1984), a pupil of Wanda Landowska, there is no historical record definitely confirming the instrument on which J. S. Bach's *The Well-Tempered Clavier* should be played. Kirkpatrick himself recorded a version on the clavichord (Archiv Produktion, 1963), then one on the harpsichord (Deutsche Grammophon 138 844/5,1967). But for this work, he preferred the clavichord.

[83] SLPM 138 537, recorded in 1962/63.

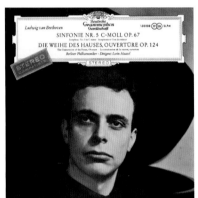

[84]

[85]

[86]

[87]

[88]

[84] … [88] A brilliant conductor and formerly a child prodigy championed by Toscanini, the American Lorin Maazel (born in 1930) was signed by Elsa Schiller at the end of the 1950s and succeeded Fricsay as the principal conductor of the Berlin Radio Symphony Orchestra. At the heart of a significant discography, the three recordings shown here, made between 1958 and 1961, are among the most beautiful of their time.

THE ARRIVAL OF STEREO . . . AND KARAJAN

But it was the birth of stereophonic sound that assured the real arrival of a modernity rich with promise. A new breakthrough in the phonographic industry, following the progression from acoustic to electric recording and from 78s to microgroove records, stereo sound became the norm for Deutsche Grammophon from 1958. Recordings made using this technology were playable on any record player available at that time. Yet for several years, many records appeared in both mono and stereo. At this time, the label had a staff of 2,000 and was producing 200,000 records per day. From 1959 the Amadeus Quartet began making their classic recordings of all of Beethoven's string quartets. Richter (Bach's *St. Matthew Passion*, 1958), August Wenzinger, then Eduard Melkus, Hanns-Martin Schneidt and the Regensburger Domspatzen (Regensburg Cathedral Choir), and the harpsichordist Ralph Kirkpatrick joined the team at Archiv; the young and brilliant Lorin Maazel, Fricsay's successor in Berlin, signed with Deutsche Grammophon.

It was at this time that Elsa Schiller achieved a great coup: Herbert von Karajan, Furtwängler's successor as principal conductor of the Berlin Philharmonic, who had defected from EMI, was welcomed into the bosom of Deutsche Grammophon. Following recordings of Dvořák, Brahms, and a dark interpretation of Strauss's *Ein Heldenleben,* the release of the first of Karajan's complete recordings of Beethoven's symphonies in 1963, played by the Berlin Philharmonic, was a real turning point. Smartly boxed, it was sold "by subscription"—an innovative marketing approach that was very successful. The recording remained an archetypal symbol of the Yellow Label and of the rise to power—artistically, aesthetically, and promotionally—of the great Austrian conductor. "The Almighty" (*Der Allmächtige*, as he was dubbed, somewhat tongue-in-cheek, by Rupert Schöttle) epitomized better than anyone the ideal, imitated, and universal figure of the modern conductor of the "glorious thirty years," as the Frenchman Jean Fourastié put it, and the German economic miracle of the postwar years. Not afraid to court controversy, English author Norman Lebrecht underlined the dubious nature of a pact between Elsa Schiller (a Jew who had been deported for nearly two years) and Karajan and Ernst von Siemens (both of whom had begun their rise to public recognition under the Nazi regime). At the same time, the two industrial giants Siemens and Philips merged their businesses in the areas of music and records into a single commercial entity: the Deutsche Grammophon Gesellschaft/Philips Phonographische Industrie (DGG/PPI), which intensified their already strong market hold.

Its catalogue may have concentrated on classic Austrian and German works, but Deutsche Grammophon looked further afield in 1961, when it established a partnership with La Scala in Milan, which brought to the record company great Italian opera performers of the time: singers (Scotto, Cossotto, Bergonzi, and Bastianini) as well as conductors (Serafin, Santini, and Gavazzeni). Verdi's operas *Un Ballo in Maschera*, *Don Carlos*, *Il Trovatore*, *La Traviata,* and *Rigoletto* (the latter conducted by Rafael Kubelik) were all recorded in the course of just a few years. In 1960, a flamboyant eighteen-year-old Argentinian pianist recorded her first recital: her name was Martha Argerich, and she remained a valuable asset for Deutsche Grammophon until after the turn of the millennium. More unexpected was the release in 1963 of a record that chronicled US president John Fitzgerald Kennedy's visit. This was during the Cold War—the wall that would cut through Berlin for twenty-eight years had been built in 1961—and the president's words "Ich bin ein Berliner" immediately made history.

[89] *Der Allmächtige*—"The Almighty": the nickname is recent, but the aura, the prestige, and the power of Herbert von Karajan (1908–1989) were evident from his first recordings on the Yellow Label in 1959. Here he is seen in rehearsal in Salzburg in 1962.

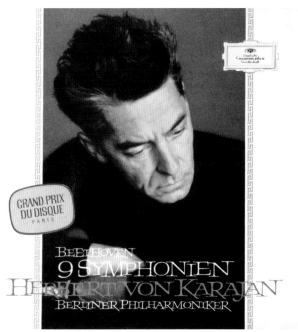

[90]…[93] The alpha and the omega of Deutsche Grammophon's catalogue, or its most enduring symbol? The first complete set of Beethoven's symphonies, which brought together Karajan and the Berlin Philharmonic, remains inscribed in letters of gold over the label's history. Its release in 1963 was an event that gave rise, for the first time, to the system of selling on subscription—even Sviatoslav Richter helped in Paris to package and distribute the precious boxes!

[90]

[91]

SUBSKRIPTION FÜR DEN DEUTSCHEN PHONOFACHHANDEL
Herausgegeben von der Deutschen Grammophon Gesellschaft

BESTELLUNG

Für.. in ....

bestelle ich hiermit nach abgeschlossener Subskription eine Sonderkassette

BEETHOVEN: NEUN SINFONIEN
Berliner Philharmoniker · Dirigent: Herbert von Karajan
in MONO / STEREO Fassung ")

Der Subskriptionspreis beträgt DM 118,– zzgl. DM 2,– für Versandspesen bei Direktversand.

Die Kassette wird von mir ausgeliefert / soll als Geschenk direkt an die umseitig angegebene Adresse geschickt werden.

Der Kunde hat den Subskriptionsausweis erhalten.

........Datum........   ....(Stempel und Unterschrift)........

") Nicht Zutreffendes bitte streichen

[92]

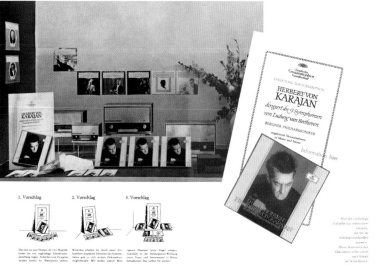

[93]

[94]

[95]

[94] [95] These Siemens company logos from 1963 show that Deutsche Grammophon was only a part of the German industrial company's music-business interests: it had been associated with the Dutch group Philips since 1962. In this photograph, taken in 1965, Ernst von Siemens can be seen leaving his Austrian subsidiary in Vienna.

[96] On the occasion of John F. Kennedy's visit to Germany in 1963, Deutsche Grammophon released the American president's Berlin speech.

[97] Having battled with illness since 1958, Ferenc Fricsay died prematurely at the age of forty-eight in 1963.

[98] [99] It was in the context of its partnership with La Scala in Milan that Deutsche Grammophon recorded Verdi's *Rigoletto* in July 1964, with Rafael Kubelik conducting, Fischer-Dieskau in the title role, and the Italian soprano Renata Scotto (1934–) in that of Gilda.

[96]

[97]

[98]

[99]

[100]

[101]

[102]

[103] Otto Gerdes (seen here in 1968 with Karajan) succeeded Elsa Schiller as Artistic Director of the label in 1963. He was also a conductor and made a notable recording of Wagner's *Tannhäuser* for Deutsche Grammophon (SLPM 139 284/87).

[103]

[100] Unique in her generation, the Argentinian pianist Martha Argerich (born in 1941) laid claim to brilliance from the moment of her first recording, made in 1960, when she was barely eighteen years old. Her love story with Deutsche Grammophon still endures.

[101] [102] Martha Argerich in Munich in January 1967, a few days after recording the Chopin album shown here (SLPM 139 317). This was also the year in which she signed her second exclusive contract, following the first in 1960.

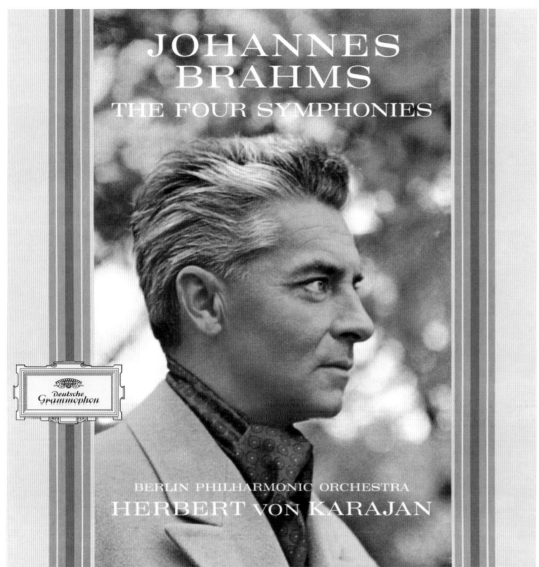

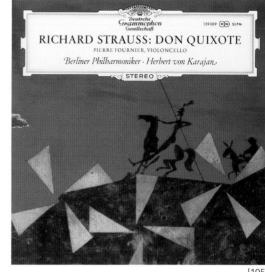

[105]

[104]

[106]

[104] Karajan's second great series for Deutsche Grammophon, the complete Brahms symphonies, released in 1964, resembles the Beethoven edition in one specific respect: the (splendid and effective) picture of the conductor has replaced that of the composer.

[105] SLPM 139 009, recorded in Berlin in 1965.

[106] Recorded the same year as Strauss's *Don Quixote*, Mascagni's *Cavalleria Rusticana* and Leoncavallo's *I Pagliacci* (SLPM 139 205/7), with La Scala in Milan, was another of Karajan's great success stories.

[107] Publicity for the release of the first audiocassettes.

MusiCassetten

[107]

[108] A rare color photograph of the Italian conductor Claudio Abbado (born in 1933) with Martha Argerich, taken during their first joint recording session in Berlin in 1967, devoted to piano concertos by Ravel and Prokofiev (SLPM 139 349).

Fricsay died prematurely in 1963, leaving unanswered a question suggested by his success; while he had no reason to envy his powerful neighbor at the Berlin Philharmonic, would the Karajan phenomenon have exercised quite so much dominance had Fricsay lived? Otto Gerdes (also a conductor) succeeded Schiller the same year: a page that, in barely ten years, had made Deutsche Grammophon a key label in the world of classical music, had turned.

TOWARD INTERNATIONALIZATION

It could be argued that from then on, the life of Deutsche Grammophon relied on the release of new recordings by Karajan, who made improvements to his work in light of even the smallest new technological developments. To cite just some of his output from the 1960s: the symphonies of Brahms; *Pagliacci* and *Cavalleria Rusticana* recorded at La Scala; some marvelous Sibelius recordings; Bruckner's Symphony no. 9; Shostakovich's Symphony no. 10; and of course Wagner's *Ring des Nibelungen,* recorded in Berlin in conjunction with his stage production at the Salzburg Easter Festival, which he founded—this is a supreme testimony to his art (Deutsche Grammophon went on to establish a presence in Salzburg, right next to the Festspielhaus). The label launched audio cassettes in 1965 and opened its recording studios to Claudio Abbado, a young Milanese conductor who had studied in Vienna. His recordings of piano concertos by Ravel and Prokofiev played by Argerich inaugurated a partnership that was representative of the new generation and of an intelligent internationalization. This was also demonstrated by Deutsche Grammophon's signing of, for example, Frenchmen Pierre Fournier, Christian Ferras, and Jean Martinon, Americans Grace Bumbry and Thomas Stewart, and the LaSalle Quartet. In 1971 the latter released a benchmark anthology of works for string quartet by Schoenberg, Berg, and Webern. Also epitomizing modernity was the shortlived "avant garde" series (twenty-four records were released between 1968 and 1971), which was devoted to the most contemporary composers: Lutoslawski, Penderecki, Kagel, Ligeti, Stockhausen, Cage, Schnebel, and Nono benefited from meticulously produced records that were distinguished by spectacularly colorful sleeves.

But this was the age of complete collections: the release in 1969 of all of Mozart's symphonies by Karl Böhm and the Berlin Philharmonic constituted another red-letter day. Begun in 1959 with Schiller and finished in 1968 with Gerdes and his soon-to-be successor Hans Hirsch, the work was a testimony to Böhm's knowledge of Mozart—released for the Austrian conductor's 75th birthday, the boxed set includes a record on which he speaks of his love of Mozart. Wagner's *Tristan und Isolde*, recorded live at Bayreuth (in 1966, with Wolfgang Windgassen and Birgit Nilsson), and Berg's *Wozzeck* and *Lulu* (which reunited Evelyn Lear and Fischer-Dieskau) were among Böhm's many other successful recordings. Other major complete recordings—the first for each composer made with Deutsche Grammophon—included Bruckner's symphonies conducted by Jochum (with the Berlin Philharmonic and the Bavarian Radio Symphony Orchestra, 1958–1966) and Mahler's symphonies conducted by Kubelik (with the Bavarian orchestra, 1967–1971). For his part, Fischer-Dieskau was happily compiling one of the most beautiful song collections ever recorded, crowned by the monumental complete recording of Schubert's lieder for male voice, with the faithful Gerald Moore at the piano, which he finished in 1972 (600 lieder on twenty-nine records sold in three boxed sets). The much-loved Fritz Wunderlich was tragically cut down on his path to glory. The Amadeus Quartet tackled Haydn, Mozart, Schubert, and Brahms. Kempff finished his second complete recording of Beethoven's

[110]

[109]

[109] [110] The French cellist Pierre Fournier (1906–1986) had a brief but brilliant career with Deutsche Grammophon. In 1953, while rehearsing Beethoven's cello sonatas in Vienna with Fournier, the Austrian pianist Friedrich Gulda (1930–2000) exclaimed, "Very beautiful, but very French," to which Fournier replied dryly, "It wasn't too French for Schnabel and Kempff." That exchange and those recording sessions resulted in a steadfast friendship.

[111] LP 2530 106, recorded in 1971 in Paris. An ambassador of French music, French conductor Jean Martinon (1910–1976) made two Lalo recordings with Deutsche Grammophon, including the famous Cello Concerto with Pierre Fournier.

[112] Frenchman Christian Ferras (1933–1982) was Karajan's favorite violinist, and they recorded several of the greatest concertos in the repertoire together. In this photograph, taken in 1967, Ferras is playing the 1728 Stradivarius Milanollo.

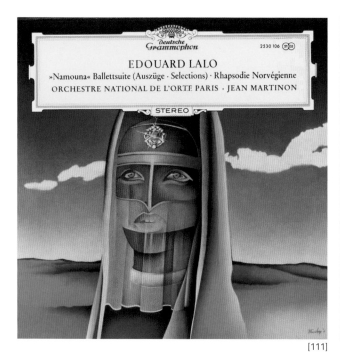

[111]

[112]

[113]

[115]

[116]

[113] [114] A pupil of Lotte Lehmann, the American mezzo-soprano Grace Bumbry (born in 1930) was the first black singer invited to perform at Bayreuth. She is seen here billed to appear in *Tannhäuser*, during which she won the nickname "Black Venus." She was also a remarkable recitalist, as was her compatriot Thomas Stewart (1928–2006), seen here rehearsing the role of Wotan with Karajan.

[115] SLPM 138 987, recorded in 1965.

[116] SLPM 138 635, recorded in 1962.

[114]

[117]

[119]

[120]

[118]

[121]

[117] Mauricio Kagel (1931–2008) composed *Exotica* in 1972 for a range of instruments unknown in the European tradition. In 1973, to celebrate its 75th anniversary, Deutsche Grammophon commissioned an original work from Kagel, which he called "1898."

[118]…[121] The five *avant garde* boxed sets (volume 2 is shown here) were dedicated to contemporary music. Many of the works recorded for this collection are today still awaiting their rerelease on CD. The Hungarian composer György Ligeti (1923–2006) took advantage of an invitation from Stockhausen to work with him in his studio in Cologne to flee his country, which had been invaded by Russian tanks in 1956. His choral work *Lux Aeterna* (recorded for Deutsche Grammophon in 1968) achieved lasting glory following its use by the filmmaker Stanley Kubrick in his film *2001: A Space Odyssey*.

[122]

[123]

[124]

[125]

[122] [123] *Tristan und Isolde* had been recorded live at the 1966 Bayreuth Festival under the direction of Karl Böhm. Wolfgang Windgassen, Eberhard Waechter, Martti Talvela (all still in costume), and Birgit Nilsson listen attentively to the first sound takes. An Isolde spanning two generations, the Swedish soprano (1918–2008) reminisced of her collaboration with Böhm: "He wasn't only a conductor who led but a man who shone."

[124] Otto Gerdes's successor, Hans Hirsch, here presents a "house" award to Karl Böhm. (The reproduction of Berliner's gramophone is recognizable.)

[125] A great Mozartian, Böhm built up a cycle of Mozart's operas between 1964 and 1979. *The Marriage of Figaro* with Hermann Prey (SLPM 139 276/79, 1968) is one of the highlights, as is *The Magic Flute*, which appeared later.

[126]

[127]

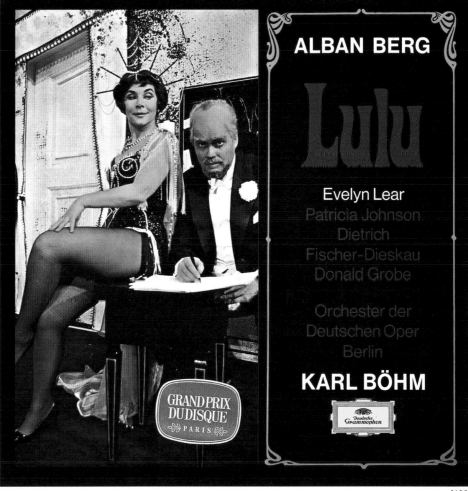

[128]

[126] Böhm's famous recording of the complete Mozart symphonies with the Berlin Philharmonic, a flagship ensemble of Deutsche Grammophon's catalogue in the 1970s, was released in 1969 to celebrate his 75th birthday.

[127] [128] The 45 rpm disc *Lear ist Lulu* is an example of an unusual, and noncommercially biased, production; it includes a radio interview with Böhm and the American soprano Evelyn Lear (born in 1926), who sang the title role in Alban Berg's opera, as well as an extract from the live recording at the Deutsche Oper Berlin in 1968 (SLPM 139 273/75). The opera's Dr. Schön is one of Fischer-Dieskau's great modern operatic roles.

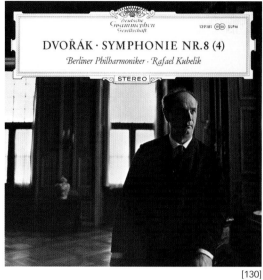

[129]

[130]

[131]

[132]

[129]…[132] Mozart by Böhm, Dvořák
by Kubelik (1914–1996), and Bruckner by
Jochum: these three major collections of
Deutsche Grammophon's catalogue at the
beginning of the 1970s gave rise to separate
editions, as seen here.

[133]

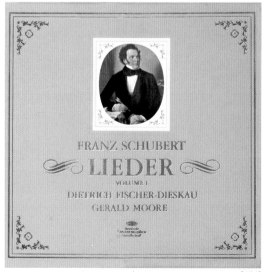

[134]

[133] [134] The English pianist Gerald Moore
(1899–1987) was Dietrich Fischer-Dieskau's
constant collaborator in building a unique
monument to Schubert: the complete
recording of all his lieder for male voice.

[135]…[137] Karl Richter and Fischer-Dieskau recording Bach's cantatas. The greatest singers under contract with Deutsche Grammophon participated in recording this cycle, but it sadly remained unfinished after Richter's premature death.

[138] German tenor Fritz Wunderlich, who died tragically in 1966, was one of the greatest singers of his time. His discography contains only memorable recordings, which happily are still available today.

[138]

[135]

[136]

[137]

[139]

[140]

[141]

[139]…[141] Publicity for the first *Beethoven Edition*, released in 1970 to celebrate the 200th anniversary of the composer's birth in Bonn. The magnificently presented boxed sets brought together the great artists in Beethoven (such as the Amadeus Quartet, top right). They also enabled the collaboration of Kempff and Menuhin, who recorded the sonatas for violin and piano together.

piano sonatas for the Yellow Label, this time in stereo (recorded in 1964–1965)—having brought to fruition, for the second time, a complete recording of Beethoven's piano concertos with Leitner in 1962 (the mono recording was with van Kempen in 1953).

In this flourishing period for the recording industry, the trend was equally as much for large-scale joint productions. Deutsche Grammophon grabbed attention almost continuously, first, by publishing in 1969–1970, for the bicentenary of the birth of Beethoven, its first *Beethoven Edition*, in collaboration with the Beethoven-Archiv in Bonn (first released on microgroove records (seventy-six of them), then on audio cassettes. The magnificent trilingual book, which accompanied the recordings, a combination of essays and accompanying illustrations, was later translated into other languages. The Beethoven Edition brought together catalogue mainstays (Karajan, Kempff, and the Amadeus Quartet) and new releases (the violin sonatas by Kempff and Yehudi Menuhin; piano trios by Kempff, Szeryng, and Fournier; and *Fidelio* by Böhm, recorded in Dresden with James King and Gwyneth Jones), as well as all of the composer's less-often performed works. Next, in 1973 and in the same vein (book included), came the no-less sumptuous edition of *The World of the Symphony* (ninety-three records in twelve boxed sets): Jochum (Haydn's "London" symphonies and Bruckner), Böhm (Mozart, Beethoven, and Schubert), Abbado (Brahms . . . with four orchestras), Karajan (Mendelssohn, Schumann, and Sibelius—the latter shared with the young Finn Okko Kamu), and Kubelik (Dvořák and Mahler) all took turns at the podium; only Tchaikovsky fell to several conductors. For its 75th anniversary, Deutsche Grammophon commissioned from Mauricio Kagel a work with the simple title *1898*. While continuing to explore Bach and German Baroque music (Karl Richter began his series of Bach cantatas in 1970), Archiv began to tackle the nineteenth century—Beethoven, Viotti, Mendelssohn, Cherubini, and Meyerbeer—in 1972. The label also released a glorious series of works by Monteverdi, Gagliano, and Schütz, entrusted to Jürgen Jürgens and his Monteverdi Choir, Hamburg (including a new *Orfeo*, sung by tenor Nigel Rogers, in 1973).

NEW PERSPECTIVES, NEW ARTISTS

Preoccupied with its desire to conquer new markets, Deutsche Grammophon had meanwhile divided its operations: the creation of PolyGram International, a supranational body with two headquarters, in Hamburg and Baarn, strengthened the partnership between Siemens and Philips that had been established in 1962. PolyGram defined itself as a holding company for an international group of companies in the leisure sector. Deutsche Grammophon GmbH became Polydor International GmbH (1971); as from 1972, the full name of Deutsche Grammophon Gesellschaft was reserved for the German branch. (This explains the disappearance of the word "Gesellschaft" from Noack's cartouche—like the tulip border, it had begun to be left off the circular record labels from the end of the 1960s.) This strategy led to the signing of an exclusive contract with the Boston Symphony Orchestra, the first US orchestra directly signed by Deutsche Grammophon (the veteran William Steinberg and the young Michael Tilson Thomas were temporarily welcomed into its fold). Even more important was the beginning of a partnership with the Vienna Philharmonic, which until then had been essentially faithful to Decca—Böhm's desire to record with his beloved Viennese orchestra had something to do with the decision, and he marked the start of the relationship with the release of a recording of Beethoven's symphonies. (This was a kind of transgression: it was the first series to challenge the undisputed supremacy of Karajan's recordings. Kubelik, Bernstein,

Böhm · Beethoven

[142]

[142] In the 1970s and 1980s, the symphonic collections recorded by Böhm in Vienna (Beethoven and Brahms) and Berlin (Mozart and Schubert) were presented in the same way as the boxed set of Beethoven's symphonies in this advertisement, which includes Böhm's final recording of the Symphony no. 9, recorded in 1980 a few months before his death.

[143] [144] It was at the beginning of the 1970s that Deutsche Grammophon embarked on its North American adventure, which was personified by William Steinberg (1899–1978) and the Boston Symphony Orchestra. The young Michael Tilson Thomas (bottom left), Claudio Abbado, and, of course, Seiji Ozawa (born in 1935) all recorded for the Yellow Label with the famous East Coast orchestra.

[143]

[144]

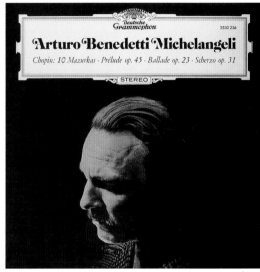

[145]

[146]

[145]…[147] There are, sometimes, unique conjunctions. At the beginning of the 1970s, Deutsche Grammophon unearthed an Italian gold mine, signing two pianists in rapid succession: Dino Ciani (1941–1974), who died shortly after having completed a memorable recording of Debussy's Préludes, among other recordings, and Arturo Benedetti Michelangeli (1920–1995), whose famous Chopin album is shown here (LP 2530 236).

[147]

[148]…[155] There had been three Italian musketeers: Ciani had died and Michelangeli was in a sense marginal, so it was left to Maurizio Pollini (born in 1942) to take over from Kempff as the label's main pianist. He has built a highly accomplished and brilliant career, combining classical and modern works. For concertos, he has collaborated with Abbado, of course—a true musical partnership (they are seen here together in 1966 in Florence)—but also with Böhm, then Jochum, with whom he recorded, with the Vienna Philharmonic, all of Beethoven's piano concertos.

[148]

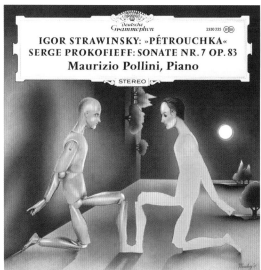

[149]

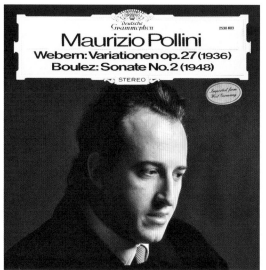

[150]

[151]

[152]

[153]

[154]

[155]

[156]

[157]

[158]

[159]

[156] [157] Carlo Maria Giulini (1914–2005) joined Deutsche Grammophon at the height of his career and recorded on both sides of the Atlantic, from Chicago to Los Angeles and Vienna to Berlin. He made, for example, a magnificent recording of Mahler's Symphony no. 9 with the Chicago Symphony Orchestra, and three Verdi sets (inaugurated by this *Rigoletto* with the Vienna Philharmonic), which still generate lively discussion today.

[158] [159] A student of the famous Japanese teacher Hideo Saito and disciple of Karajan, the Japanese conductor Seiji Ozawa is at home with many styles, but particularly French (Berlioz, Ravel, and Poulenc) and Romantic (Tchaikovsky and Prokofiev) music. After Ozawa's success at the International Competition for Young Conductors in Besançon in 1959, Charles Munch invited him to conduct the Boston Symphony Orchestra, of which he later served as musical director, from 1973 to 2002.

and Abbado—three times—and Gardiner followed suit over the years.) In anticipation of the 25th anniversary of Archiv (which had been managed by Andreas Holschneider since 1970), releases in 1970 and 1971 of the second complete recording of organ works by Bach was arranged, played by the great Walcha—fifteen records in two boxed sets. But it was the appearance of artists from other cultures that marked the beginning of the new decade. The arrival on the Yellow Label of Italian pianists Arturo Benedetti-Michelangeli (particularly renowned for his interpretations of Chopin and Debussy), Dino Ciani (who, tragically, was killed in an accident), and of course Maurizio Pollini, showed the flair of Hans Hirsch, who held the post of Head of Production until 1982. Pollini was renowned for his performances of many twentieth-century works over the years (Stravinsky, Prokofiev, Schoenberg, Webern, Nono, Boulez, Stockhausen, and Manzoni), as well as concerto recordings with Jochum, Böhm, and, of course, Abbado, a true musical brother. Seiji Ozawa and Carlo Maria Giulini also joined Deutsche Grammophon, and over the years recorded a large part of their preferred repertoires (Tchaikovsky, Prokofiev, and French music in Ozawa's case; Schubert, Bruckner, Brahms, Mahler, and autumnal, uncut versions of *Rigoletto*, *Il Trovatore,* and *Falstaff* in Giulini's). But Karajan remained the all-powerful king—and Deutsche Grammophon marketed this image of him everywhere. They had never offered anyone else so much. Over and above his standard interpretations (Strauss, still, including a splendid *Four Last Songs* with Gundula Janowitz, Mozart, Brahms, and Bruckner) was the memorable anthology that he dedicated in 1974 to the Second Viennese School—a new move for him. This was a bewitching collection that seemed to have been created by Klingsor, recorded with the Berlin Philharmonic during the years that marked the high point of their collaboration. Contrasted with this, the return to his favorite scores, especially Beethoven (his second complete recording with the Berlin Philharmonic, 1975–1977, was released for the 150th anniversary of the composer's death) and Brahms (*idem*, 1977–1978), though they helped to establish his ubiquity, almost gave the impression of repetition—but there was no question that the new recordings were of outstanding quality.

And yet some other remarkable artists emerged in this landscape, not to steal Karajan's crown, but to broaden music's horizons. Leonard Bernstein arrived on the scene in 1972, with an exotic *Carmen* from the Metropolitan Opera of New York (with Marilyn Horne and James McCracken), Liszt's *Faust* Symphony (which was coupled with the prologue to Boïto's *Mefistofele*), and a Beethoven benefit concert for Amnesty International with Claudio Arrau, signs of what was to come. In the meantime, an ageless maverick made a sudden entrance: his name was Carlos Kleiber, the son of Erich, who had cut some valuable records with Deutsche Grammophon before he emigrated in 1935, antagonized by Nazi harassment. In 1973, in Dresden, Carlos recorded Weber's *Der Freischütz* (with Gundula Janowitz and Peter Schreier) with supreme freedom as well as control; a stunning interpretation of Beethoven's Symphony no. 5, then his no. 7, Brahms's Symphony no. 4—all with the Vienna Philharmonic—Johann Strauss II's *Die Fledermaus*, and Verdi's *La Traviata* followed. Each was a success, but Kleiber was an elusive character, anxious and dissatisfied, capable of abandoning a project even at the studio door or of refusing to release a recorded album even when it was already "in the can." This self-critical strictness was part of what made him a legend.

[160]

[161]

Schönberg·Berg·Webern
Berliner Philharmoniker
Herbert von Karajan

[162]

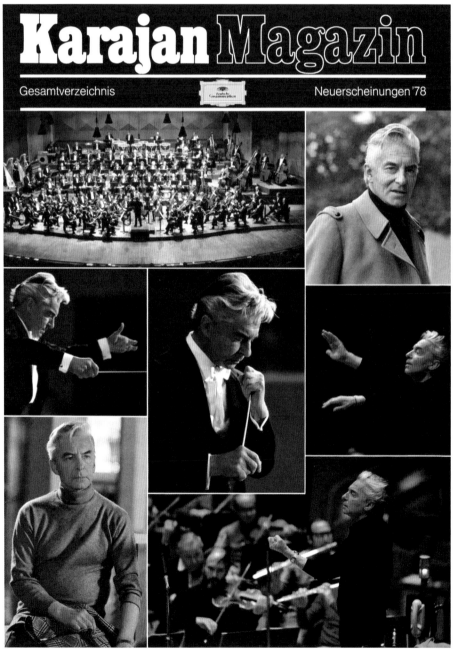

[163]

[160]…[163] A magazine devoted only to Karajan? Its cover portrays a carefully constructed image, with photographs that are very precisely studied, posed, and controlled. But the musician didn't sacrifice quality for the glamour of stardom. His later collection of works by the Second Viennese School are counted among his greatest recordings for the Yellow Label. German soprano Gundula Janowitz (born in 1937) was one of the singers with whom Karajan collaborated most closely: Haydn, Mozart, Beethoven, Brahms, Wagner, and Strauss often brought them together.

[164]

BEETHOVEN · BERNSTEIN
Symphony No.5 · Piano Concerto No.4 · Overture Leonore III
Bavarian Radio Symphony Orchestra
CLAUDIO ARRAU, Piano

[165]

[166]

[164]…[166] Deutsche Grammophon may not have imagined, in the early days, the place that would eventually be taken by American pianist, conductor, and teacher Leonard Bernstein (seen here, typically, with cigarette in hand and surrounded by people, during a recording session for *Carmen*, his first production for the label). He was bearded only for a short time, as here in 1976, at the concert held in Munich with Claudio Arrau in aid of Amnesty International.

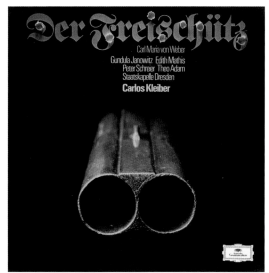

[167]

[168]

[169]

[170]

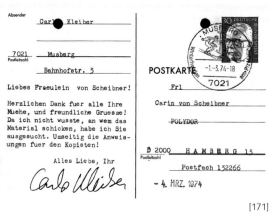

[171]

[167]…[171] Another unique talent, Carlos Kleiber (1930–2004) was as private and elusive as Bernstein was open and forthcoming. Made in less than ten years, the albums he recorded for Deutsche Grammophon can be counted on the fingers of two hands. All bear the blazing, agile mark of this dazzling performer.

[172]

[173]

[174]

[172] French publicity for the *Bach Edition*, published by Archiv Produktion. Its release was a big event: the edition comprised a large part of the Archiv catalogue recorded over the previous twenty years. This edition has evolved over the years to include (in its CD counterpart) recordings using early instruments.

[173] David Munrow (1942–1976): the great specialist in medieval and Renaissance music was commissioned by Deutsche Grammophon, a year before his suicide, to record an anthology of music from the Gothic era with his ensemble, the Early Music Consort of London.

[174] Abbado reclaimed Deutsche Grammophon's Verdi tradition, which dated back to Caruso and Schlusnus. His brilliant *Macbeth* gave rise to a significant series, often with Domingo.

In 1974 Deutsche Grammophon began releasing the greatest masterpieces of chamber music in the *Privilege* series. The following year, Archiv Produktion assembled its Bach catalogue in a *Bach Edition*, commemorating the 225th anniversary of the composer's death. The eleven silver-colored boxes containing ninety-nine records (on which Richter and Walcha were omnipresent), were supplemented with erudite presentation notes—a constant feature with Archiv. Essays and illustrations were brought together in a German-English volume, published by Bärenreiter. Archiv also released an anthology *Music of the Gothic Era*, entrusted to David Munrow and his Early Music Consort of London, which in 1975 marked the start of a vast program devoted to the music of different eras, schools, and genres: it led to the signing of many specialist ensembles (for example, the Pro Cantione Antiqua of London and Camerata Bern). Charles Mackerras, meanwhile, was put in charge of some original projects, such as Mozart's version of Handel's *Messiah,* 1974. In 1976, with a splendid *Macbeth* (with Shirley Verrett and Piero Cappuccilli), Abbado inaugurated a series of recordings of Verdi operas with La Scala, rejuvenating the project undertaken in the 1960s.

Another highly self-critical performer of utmost musical integrity joined Deutsche Grammophon very young, in the wake of his success at the international Chopin competition in Warsaw: the Polish pianist Krystian Zimerman (Chopin and Mozart were his first offerings). Discovered by Karajan, violinist Anne-Sophie Mutter, an even younger musician, made her recording debut of Mozart in 1978, and she was soon followed by Gidon Kremer, another original and inspired artist. In 1977 Archiv signed a long-term contract with Musica Antiqua of Cologne and its leader Reinhard Goebel; Trevor Pinnock and the English Concert (Bach, Handel, and Purcell) and John Eliot Gardiner and the two ensembles of his creation, the English Baroque Soloists and the Monteverdi Choir (*Acis and Galatea*, 1978; *The Fairy Queen*, 1981; and *Hercules*, 1982) followed suit. Stylistically erudite and artistically sophisticated, their exemplary musical achievements gave Archiv a new impetus. Once again, the Hamburg company had known how to interpret the times. But it now found itself on the eve of a dual revolution: digital recording and, following in its wake, the appearance of the CD.

[175]

[176]

[177]

[175]…[177] Make way for youth! The end of the 1970s saw the appearance of some new faces. The Polish pianist Krystian Zimerman (born in 1956) and especially the German violinist Anne-Sophie Mutter (born in 1963) benefited from Karajan's attentive support. Mutter remains an inviolable figure of Deutsche Grammophon's catalogue, in which she made her first appearance in 1978 with the recording of Mozart's two most famous violin concertos.

[178] [179] Zimerman won the prestigious international Chopin piano competition in Warsaw in 1975. This photograph shows him with Giulini, with whom he recorded Chopin's two piano concertos in 1978. A very demanding and often unsatisfied performer, he rerecorded them in 1999, this time leading from the piano an orchestra of young Polish musicians that he had handpicked. Released for the 150th anniversary of Chopin's death, it was a huge success.

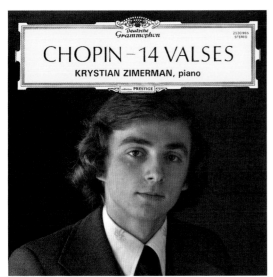

[178]

[179]

[180]

[181]

[182]

[180]…[182] The spirit of Woodstock applied to classical music, or rather Baroque and preclassical: Musica Antiqua of Cologne and its inspirational founder, Reinhard Goebel (the violinist wearing a T-shirt), performed German and Italian music with a previously unknown vigor and rawness, giving the Archiv label a momentum that has endured and opening up new horizons. The same was true of Trevor Pinnock (1946–) and The English Concert in their own, much more English, style. Pinnock— here looking strangely medieval—is a magnificent harpsichordist who has recorded some beautiful solo albums (Bach, Handel, and Telemann).

DR. ANDREAS HOLSCHNEIDER
Former President of Deutsche Grammophon
Former Director of Archiv Produktion

You were the director of Archiv Produktion from 1970, then assumed control of the classical division of Polydor in 1981, and were Deutsche Grammophon's president until 1992. How would you define Deutsche Grammophon?
I think that Deutsche Grammophon is a company with a strong reputation. This reputation is based on four pillars—artistic quality, technical knowledge, design, and promotion—and, finally, the label. The Yellow Label was created in 1949, so it is younger than the company, which was created in 1898. The yellow cartouche was created in 1958 and is now fifty-one years old. The label shows exactly what Deutsche Grammophon is: a company that records classical music exclusively, is German, and manufactures in Germany.

How did Deutsche Grammophon survive after the Second World War?
Deutsche Grammophon had a very difficult time, especially between 1936 and 1946. The time of the war, and the years just before it, were extremely difficult for the company, which even went into liquidation in 1937. It has survived nevertheless. When Siemens took over the company in 1941, it started up again but was once more defeated by the war. In 1945 the opera houses, the recording studio, and the factories in Hanover were destroyed, and the orchestras were disintegrating, so we had nothing. Moreover, under the Third Reich, Deutsche Grammophon was very much under the shadow of the political regime. Nevertheless, it is clear that Deutsche Grammophon was interested primarily in working with great artists. Karajan first became a leading figure of Deutsche Grammophon before the war, and Furtwängler also recorded for Deutsche Grammophon. But after the war, the situation was disastrous, because the great artists had either emigrated and signed contracts with other companies or were not authorized to record and perform anymore. How could we show the technological quality of this "reborn company"? Without artists, it was difficult! So Deutsche Grammophon decided to focus on what others did not have: early German music, composed by Bach's predecessors and by Bach himself. That is how the Archiv label was born. At that time, Bach was the most played composer. In Bach people could find the soul that they had lost during the war. So Archiv was founded for cultural reasons but also for marketing ones. In the first few years after the war, Archiv's productions represented more than a third of the company's total output.

Why was it not until the 1960s that Deutsche Grammophon became a real "opera label?"
The company had not been ready beforehand, because of the aftermath of the Second World War. Deutsche Grammophon started to become an opera label when Karl Böhm began to record the Strauss operas. Herbert von Karajan, who was the leading figure of Deutsche Grammophon from the 1960s until his death, founded the Salzburg Easter Festival in 1967. Before that, he was at La Scala, in Milan, and in Vienna. He was also the head of the great Salzburg Summer Festival. So, from the 1960s, Deutsche Grammophon became a great opera label. I agree that, until then, Decca had been *the* opera label. With

Böhm, Karajan, and, later, Abbado, Bernstein, Giulini, Sinopoli, Ozawa, Levine, and many others, this situation changed.

How did Herbert von Karajan influence Deutsche Grammophon's catalogue?

Karajan came back to Deutsche Grammophon in 1959. From then until his death, thirty years later, he made about 330 recordings—that's more than ten discs a year. He was really a record man. He was connected with the Berlin Philharmonic, of course, but also with the Vienna Philharmonic and the Vienna Opera. He was the creator of his own festival and the chairman of the Salzburg Festival. And everything that he did was represented in either Deutsche Grammophon's catalogue or EMI's. His work is a kind of a mirror of the European festival culture of that time.

From the 1960s, and more intensively in the 1970s, Deutsche Grammophon started signing contracts with international conductors and became an international label . . .

That's right, but more fundamentally, the reason that Deutsche Grammophon really became an international label was its global distribution. The uniting of Philips, Decca, and Deutsche Grammophon under PolyGram led to the internationalization of our company. For instance, Japan was the second market after Germany for us, but with PolyGram, the United States became a very important market, too. So besides the internationalization of our artists, that distribution gave Deutsche Grammophon its international success. Because the product itself—classical music—is international.

How were Deutsche Grammophon's covers conceived?

Deutsche Grammophon was privileged to have some outstanding art directors. In particular, Pali Meller Marcovicz was, for more than thirty years, an important figure in our company. He was the man who discussed with Karajan and all the other great artists how to present their recordings. It was Pali, with his team, who created the covers, designed the booklets, and conceived the best way to present and promote the recordings. He helped to establish the reputation that Deutsche Grammophon has had since then for high-quality visuals. He would constantly highlight the central place of the yellow cartouche, which at that time occupied as much as 25 percent of the covers of high-price LPs. Other companies do not have this kind of cartouche, which is a trademark stating that Deutsche Grammophon produces only classical music. And the visual identity symbolized by the yellow cartouche is extremely strong. Moreover, the process of selecting pictures was rigorous, and the pictures chosen were serious ones. I remember when Leonard Bernstein came to Deutsche Grammophon: he wanted to be seen as a German, music-making artist; he wanted to change his image, that is to say, to be seen as European. He came to us because we had the German heritage necessary for German repertoire. He was trying to find a way into Europe and, with the help of Deutsche Grammophon, he was able to become part of the established European musical tradition.

And similarly, it was very important for Deutsche Grammophon's image to have Leonard Bernstein . . .

It was a wonderful thing. What would "German" mean without its connection to its Jewish past? It was extremely important, and having Leonard Bernstein and other Jewish artists opened new directions for this German company.

How did you prepare for the future?

Well, there was a conductor ten years younger than Herbert von Karajan: Leonard Bernstein. There was a conductor fifteen years younger than Bernstein: Claudio Abbado. There was a conductor thirteen years younger than Claudio Abbado: Giuseppe Sinopoli. New generations followed on. So we were not unprepared. We signed a contract with Carlo Maria Giulini, who was a very important conductor, not only for Italian repertoire but also because he was well versed in German culture and musical heritage. Carlos Kleiber recorded some tremendous operas: *La Traviata, Der Freischütz, Die Fledermaus,* and *Tristan und Isolde.* And it is certain that if Kleiber had wanted—if he had shown interest—he could have been Karajan's successor in Berlin. Nobody could have foreseen that Bernstein would die only one year after Karajan. Nobody could have imagined that Claudio Abbado would fall severely ill. Nobody could have guessed that Sinopoli would die so young in 2001. Or that Kleiber would die three years later. So we were prepared for the future, and not only with conductors but also with regard to other parts of our catalogue, with Anne-Sophie Mutter, Krystian Zimerman, Gil Shaham, the Hagen Quartet, and many others.

In the 1990s, the situation was nevertheless much more difficult for Deutsche Grammophon . . .
Yes, but not because we were unprepared. When I left Deutsche Grammophon in 1992, we had a 25 percent share of the whole market for classical music! Decca and Philips shared another 25 percent. So in total, PolyGram had 50 percent of the market, half of which was held by Deutsche Grammophon. Today, the market share is the same, but the turnover has dropped dramatically. The market crumbled because the medium was exhausted; the CD was exhausted, just as the LP had been at the end of the 1970s. Everything had already been recorded, many times over. You cannot keep rerecording the whole repertoire unless you can do so with a new technology that will add something radically new. Moreover, the sales went down, because people had other interests and access to music through the Internet. In addition, the team who had been running Deutsche Grammophon left: Günther Breest, Pali Meller Marcovicz, Hanno Rinke, Antje Henneking, the leading figures of the Emile Berliner Studios . . . so I think that the firm needed time to reconstruct a new team identity, a new coherence with new people.

Has Deutsche Grammophon's artistic policy changed from that time?
I think so. It has become virtually impossible to conduct a repertoire policy today in the way we used to. Today, the focus is on artists, which really means stars. Of course, this was also the case fifty years ago. We used to say, "Deutsche Grammophon is the label for the stars and the label is a star." At that time, it was principal for us to combine this focus on stars with a repertoire policy. But the repertoire is limited. Classical repertoire means Bach to Richard Strauss. As I said, everything has already been recorded, and many times. Do not forget that there is only a market if there is a new medium. This is the problem. Because it's all been done already, and wonderfully well. That is why I think that focusing on stars is the only way forward today. Deutsche Grammophon created new anthologies, new editions in the past, but these are becoming more and more obsolete. An artistic policy that focuses on stars is what is in demand today. And Deutsche Grammophon manages this well!

ALFRED KAINE
Former repertoire manager for Deutsche Grammophon

You dedicated the major part of your career at Deutsche Grammophon to its repertoire development. How did your collaboration with the company start?
I was a *répétiteur* and conductor associated with various ballet companies and theaters in the United States and two opera houses in Germany before applying to Deutsche Grammophon for a job in 1968. One of my main reasons for doing so was that I have always been fascinated by the history and traditions of the recording industry in general and that of the old Gramophone Company in particular. I began my life at Deutsche Grammophon as a product manager on September 1, 1968. In the autumn of 1978, I transferred to A&R, and in 1986 I officially went back to product management, but actually functioned in both departments until my retirement at the end of 1993. My title was Repertoire Manager, which first included managing the back catalogue, including historical reissues, and then branching out into direct marketing and special projects. Coming from the musical side, there was no better way of learning the balance between the musical and commercial aspects of the job. My work developed into creating editions, recommending recordings for new artists or for contracts that had been extended, assessing and acquiring repertoire from outside sources, and a great deal of studio work, which I loved doing.

What was Elsa Schiller's influence on Deutsche Grammophon's artist roster?
Deutsche Grammophon had the enormous luck of having found Elsa Schiller after the war. With astute knowledge, she reconstructed the firm, building up a roster of artists, such as Wilhelm Kempff, Ferenc Fricsay, Eugen Jochum, Karl Böhm, Igor Markevitch, Wolfgang Schneiderhan, and many others, including Karl Richter and Ralph Kirkpatrick on Archiv, creating a catalogue that was both multifaceted and attractive. It was she who grasped the opportunity to record Wilhelm Furtwängler in 1951/52, during a break between his EMI contracts. The atmosphere at these legendary recordings (of Schubert's Symphony no. 9, Haydn's Symphony no. 88, Schumann's Symphony No. 4 and Furtwängler's own Symphony no. 2), encouraged Furtwängler (and later Karajan) again to record with his own Berlin Philharmonic, which was under contract to Deutsche Grammophon. The atmosphere was so positive that Furtwängler would very likely have switched to Deutsche Grammophon in September 1957, when his last contract with EMI was to have ended. Alas, he died on November 30, 1954. It was Elsa Schiller who, in 1959, built bridges with Herbert von Karajan, who had left EMI, leading to the unique recordings of Beethoven's nine symphonies in 1962/63. With the release of these symphonies as a boxed set and as individual LP issues, the idea of editions was born, creating a marketing sensation.

You worked a lot on historical recordings . . .
I inherited the historical series soon after I entered the firm. It was a subject that interested me greatly, as did the entire background of the firm. I also considered it my duty to find shellac copies of recordings made for us by artists who were either Jewish, such as Alexander Kipnis, Otto Klemperer, and Bruno Walter, or anti-Nazi, such as Lotte Lehmann and Adolf and Fritz Busch. Another banned artist who made many Deutsche Grammophon recordings was Frida Leider;

she saved her Jewish husband by not leaving him, but her career was for all intents finished and her recordings were banned. Curiously, the matrices for a single recording of each such artist were saved, despite the directive from the Nazis to destroy the discs or submit them for melting down. In the case of Erich Kleiber, it was Dvořák's *New World* Symphony; in that of Klemperer, it was two Beethoven overtures and Kurt Weill's *Kleine Dreigroschenmusik*. I don't remember which recordings of Lotte Lehmann survived. As a result of my searches, I was able to reissue a number of recordings, but there were many, such as those by Bruno Walter, dating from the acoustic era, and those of Fritz Busch, that I never found.

Another facet of my work with historical recordings was with those of Wilhelm Furtwängler. I had been raised in the United States with the stringent interpretations of Arturo Toscanini, so Furtwängler's way of phrasing and breathing was a revelation to me. In the 1960s Deutsche Grammophon acquired the rights to a number of Reichsrundfunk recordings, and I was very happy to supplement this catalogue with a large number of additional recordings, both from the war years and afterward.

What is the most significant memory of your career in the company?
I had put together the absolutely complete *Beethoven Edition* in 1992 and 1993, planning it in compositional blocks that made sense and CDs that would provide absorbing listening and were practical commercially. I had the great luck to work with the wonderful Beethoven musicologist Dr. Nicholas Marston. When the program had been put together, I flew over to England to meet Nick at Cambridge University, where he still teaches today, to clear up details regarding versions of various works and to answer other questions. The suite *WoO 33*, which was put together by a publisher, comes to mind in this respect. We worked in the quiet of the awe-inspiring library with its enormous history. Whenever there was a question that needed answering, there were replicas of the original manuscripts in the archives below the main hall. We were allowed to work totally uninterrupted, which for me was almost unknown. Seldom have I experienced such a feeling of awe, atmospheric inspiration, and deep satisfaction.

[01]

1979–2010
RÉMY LOUIS

The arrival of digital technology, and then of the CD (compact disc), came just at the right moment to rescue the record industry from the slump that was facing it at the end of the 1970s. Hermann Franz, technical director of Deutsche Grammophon since 1978, was responsible for the company's CD planning and development, which took several years, although the first digital recording (Tchaikovsky's Violin Concerto, performed by Gidon Kremer and the Berlin Philharmonic and conducted by Lorin Maazel) was made in 1979. But this was still a time of reorganization: the "classical" departments of Deutsche Grammophon and Philips were split from their American subsidiaries to become a separate entity, PolyGram Classics International. However, each retained command of its artistic and editorial decisions (they were joined by the English label Decca after its acquisition in 1980), an autonomy that was also enjoyed by the national subsidiaries under the PolyGram Classics label. From then on, the "recording" business of Polydor International and Phonogram International came under PolyGram Records Operations.

THE ARRIVAL OF THE COMPACT DISC

A recording made in Paris by Pierre Boulez accompanied this transition: Berg's *Lulu* (with Teresa Stratas and Franz Mazura, 1979), the unfinished third act of which had been completed by Friedrich Cerha. Two important new artists were signed: the Italian conductor and composer Giuseppe Sinopoli, who began with a recording dedicated to his compatriot Bruno Maderna (*Quadrivium*, *Aura*, and *Biogramma*, 1979), and American pianist and conductor James Levine (Schumann's Piano Quintet with the LaSalle Quartet, 1980).

The role that they would play was witness to the irreversible internationalization of the Yellow Label—over the years, they recorded numerous opera collections with some of the greatest names of the operatic world. The supremacy of the Austro-German artists that had formed the backbone of Deutsche Grammophon's reputation from the period between the two world wars until the 1960s waned; Karl Richter and Karl Böhm both died in 1981. But the turning point that year was the international presentation of the CD at the Salzburg Easter Festival; developed by Philips and Sony, it would be manufactured by PolyGram at its Hanover-Langenhagen factory.

The changes in sound reproduction that the CD brought about were radical: linked to advancements in computer technology, the CD is based on a digital process. The principle consists of encoding the sound message in billions of numbers, rather than retaining an analog copy of a vibration, which had been the case since the early days of the record. It was no longer about grooves. A CD comprises billions of long and short indentations, called pits, each no more than .002 mm in width. The CD player—in reality a computer—is capable of reconstituting even the most complex numbers at the rate of several million operations per second. These numbers correspond to encoded signals, relating to subtleties of tone, pitch, and volume, which are initially picked up by the sound recording. Once the message has been decoded, the CD player transforms it into an electric current that is transmitted to loudspeakers via a traditional stereo amplifier. The disc is read by means of a laser: directed onto the pits moving in front of it, it is reflected from them through a prism to the computer, which then decodes the signals from the pits. In contrast to records, CDs are scanned from interior to exterior, the speed gradually decreasing (from 500 to 200 rpm) to preserve a constant running speed.

It is an interesting historical fact that the 12 cm diameter of the new medium was identical, to within a few millimeters, to that of Emile Berliner's first records! It is said that the CD's nominal duration (which was rapidly extended), was determined by the recording of Beethoven's Symphony no. 9 with which Furtwängler reopened the Bayreuth Festival in 1951—apparently the work was a suggestion by Karajan. He was enthusiastic about the new format, which led him to revisit for the last time the heart of his repertoire. But he added titles that were absent from his previous recordings for Deutsche Grammophon, all well suited to highlight the most technical performances: Strauss's Alpine Symphony, the first mass-produced CD (1982), and Saint-Saëns's *Organ* Symphony. It went without saying that Karajan was the first ambassador of the new medium. Leaving Archiv, Andreas Holschneider became the head of Polydor International's classical division.

The year 1981 also witnessed the arrival of the fiery pianist Ivo Pogorelich, whose cause had been taken up by Argerich, and of the great Rudolf Serkin, then in his twilight years. (His legacy includes Beethoven's late piano sonatas, Brahms's cello sonatas with Rostropovich, and several of Mozart's piano concertos with Abbado.) The centenary of the Berlin Philharmonic (1982) gave rise to an edition of six boxed sets of records that also summarized, in part, the history of Deutsche Grammophon. But another orchestral king of Germany's musical scene was covered with glory in the same year: the Dresden Staatskapelle was chosen by Kleiber to record an impressive *Tristan und Isolde* (with Margaret Price and René Kollo)—unfortunately, his last official recording under the Yellow Label.

[02]

[01] The compact disc, released in 1981, and its ancestor invented by Emile Berliner at the end of the nineteenth century. Interestingly, these two media have almost the same diameter with a difference of only a few millimeters.

[02] Gidon Kremer is an original violinist, an inspired artist and a musician who is curious about everything and everyone, whether he is performing as a soloist, with a chamber ensemble, or in front of an orchestra.

[03]…[06] Two very different personalities, one very American, the other very attached to the middle-European tradition, conductors James Levine (born in 1943) and Giuseppe Sinopoli (1946–2001) left their mark on Deutsche Grammophon's catalogue in many ways: Levine is also a magnificent pianist and Sinopoli was an esteemed composer (and psychoanalyst).

[03]

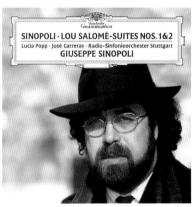

[04]

[06]

[05]

[07]

[08]

[09]

[07]…[09] *Lulu* again? Yes, but with the third act completed by Friedrich Cerha. The premiere of this version in Paris in 1979 made headlines around the world. An admirer of Pierre Boulez (born in 1925), Böhm would have liked him to have been the one to complete the orchestration of *Lulu*. Böhm died in the same year (1981) as Karl Richter, who is seen here receiving an award from Andreas Holschneider: "The 1970s are blotted out" (to use the title of a paper by German writer Ernst Jünger).

[10] [11] Art and industry come together under the banners of new technology and progress. Herbert von Karajan could not let the CD revolution pass him by: here, he is seen with Akio Morita, Sony's founder, at the international launch of the CD during the Salzburg Easter Festival of 1981.

[11]

[12]

[13]

[14]

[15]

[12] [13] The International Frederyk Chopin Piano Competition in Warsaw has given Deutsche Grammophon several of its exclusive artists: Maurizio Pollini (winner in 1960), Martha Argerich (1965), and Krystian Zimerman (1975). In 1980, the label engaged not the competition's winner, but rather the young Yugoslavian pianist Ivo Pogorelich, whose unconventional style had divided the jury. Argerich, a jury member, subsequently took up his cause. Chopin was clearly on the bill for his first recording for Deutsche Grammophon, which this time divided the critics.

[14] [15] The label's discography of Austrian-born pianist Rudolf Serkin (1903–1991) has remained limited, the company having signed him in later life. It comprises the last Beethoven piano sonatas, Brahms's cello sonatas with Mstislav Rostropovich (1927–2007), and a significant number of Mozart's piano concertos with Claudio Abbado.

[16] In 1982 the Berlin Philharmonic's centenary provided Deutsche Grammophon with an opportunity to revisit its own past, which has so often been linked with that of the legendary orchestra. Dating back to some acoustic recordings, the first boxed set in the collection, shown here, magnificently presented this joint history.

[16]

The 150th anniversary in 1983 of the birth of Brahms was celebrated with the release of recordings of his complete works, sold, as became the proven formula, with the addition of a trilingual book that was later published by German music publisher Breitkopf & Härtel. The development of the catalogue gave rise to the appearance of themed series (for example *Signature* focused on performers), though these were subject to a few changes of name, or even to a different editorial slant, from one country to another.

BERNSTEIN FOREVER

The internal reorganizations continued: in 1983, the year that the CD was launched across Europe, the classical division of Polydor International took the name of Deutsche Grammophon International, while remaining under the ownership of PolyGram International; and the three sources of classical repertoire (Decca in London, Deutsche Grammophon in Hamburg, and Philips in Baarn) were placed under the sole leadership of PolyGram Classics International, though the unique character of each was retained. The following year, Siemens sold 40 percent of the half shares it held in PolyGram International to Philips (which acquired the remaining 10 percent in 1987). Many recordings appeared in the early 1980s, in three formats: LP, CD, and audiocassette. The latter format gained its independence (and brought in a lot of money) following an agreement with Sony that resulted in *Walkman Classics*, released specifically on this medium (a chromium-dioxide tape with a playing time of one-and-one-half hours). Karajan recorded his third series of Beethoven's symphonies (1984), digitally and on CD, as was to be expected, followed by a final series of Brahms's symphonies (not counting the video recordings). His visit to the Vatican with the Vienna Philharmonic resulted, in 1985, in a recording of Mozart's *Coronation Mass*, performed in front of Pope John Paul II. But from then on, other conductors—Abbado, Barenboim, Sinopoli, and Levine—infiltrated his realm more noticeably: the symphonies of Schumann and Bruckner by Barenboim with the Chicago Symphony Orchestra, those of Beethoven by Abbado with the Vienna Philharmonic (1986–1989), and Wagner's *Ring des Nibelungen* by Levine (1987–1989) with the Metropolitan Opera of New York represent this trend. Levine also brought to fruition his recording of the complete symphonies of Mozart, which, curiously, was the only one completed at that time by the Vienna Philharmonic. In the long run, however, no one encroached more on Karajan's territory than Leonard Bernstein: in just over ten years, from 1977 to 1988, he gave Deutsche Grammophon, with the Vienna Philharmonic, series of recordings of Beethoven, Brahms, Mozart and Schumann. And he ruled unchallenged in Mahler—even though Karajan, a circumspect latecomer to Mahler, bequeathed two otherworldly recordings of his Symphony no. 9, in the studio then live, following a poignant *Parsifal* released in 1981.

Bernstein also rerecorded almost all of his own works for Deutsche Grammophon. As he had hoped, the recording of *West Side Story* (1985) brought together the opera singers Kiri Te Kanawa and José Carreras. Astonishingly, this was the first time that he had conducted his masterpiece in its entirety; its success was highlighted by the television documentary that was shot during the recording sessions. Could his presence on the Yellow Label have been imagined fifteen years previously? 1985 also saw Deutsche Grammophon sign another US legend, the pianist Vladimir Horowitz (of whom the label was legitimately proud): "the last romantic" came back long enough to add several CDs of his usual repertoire, and also moved into some unexpected territory at this stage of his career—Schubert's Piano Sonata, D. 960 in B Major and, especially, Mozart's Piano Concerto no. 23, with Giulini.

[17]

[19]

[17] [18] It is possible for the pursuit of higher distribution figures (for example, thanks to the Walkman) to go hand in hand with the quest for spirituality? Like many Austro-German conductors, Herbert von Karajan traveled to the Vatican during the pontificate of Paul VI, then again in 1985 during that of John Paul II. The audio and video recordings of this solemn occasion (Mozart's *Coronation Mass*) were released shortly afterward.

[19] Always spurred on by his passion for progress, Karajan advanced along his Beethovenian path until his dying day. Shown here is his third complete recording of the symphonies.

[18]

LEONARD BERNSTEIN · VIENNA PHILHARMONIC

[21]

[20] [21] For his European public, and for the heads of Deutsche Grammophon, Leonard Bernstein embodied a new way of living and communicating music that was universally appealing. In just a few years, the American artist had built up a tremendous catalogue, mainly with the Vienna and Israel Philharmonic Orchestras. He changed the course of classical recording, and was, himself, transformed in the process.

[22]

[23]

[22] The premiere of *West Side Story* took place in New York in 1957. At the piano was the famous Stephen Sondheim, who wrote the lyrics for the musical.

[23] In 1984, again in New York, Bernstein, at the podium, goes over the music one last time with his soloists and singers, in his obsessive desire to please and be pleased. The result is irresistible but rehearsals were not pain free, as is shown in the film that was shot during recording sessions, which lasted a week.

[24]

[25]

[24] Karajan's "official" photographer, Siegfried Lauterwasser (1913–2000), took photographs of Karajan's recording sessions; a contact sheet is shown here.

[25] This picture of Bernstein lost in thought was used for the cover of the conductor's complete Mahler recording.

Interview with Olivier Boruchowitch. Translation: Alexander Holliday. Photo: private collection

BERNSTEIN AND DEUTSCHE GRAMMOPHON: A UNIQUE MARRIAGE
BY HANNO RINKE

Former Vice President of International Marketing for Deutsche Grammophon
Leonard Bernstein's Producer

You joined Deutsche Grammophon in 1969 then became product manager for New Releases, head of the Repertoire Office, director of the Video Department and vice president for International Marketing, before leaving the company in 1993 to set up your own television studio. From 1978 you were Leonard Bernstein's executive producer. How did you get him to sign on as an exclusive Deutsche Grammophon artist?

We made him an offer he could not refuse. By the late 1970s Bernstein had recorded almost all of the repertoire that interested him with CBS. To Americans, he was synonymous with classical music, but the market was oversaturated. To Europeans, he was "the American" who, in addition to writing musicals, performed classical music. The task I saw before me was to reintroduce the Europeans to Bernstein, to the wider person they did not know. My American Deutsche Grammophon colleagues' response to this idea was, "Good luck, but don't count on us!"

This strategy rested on three pillars: first, the Viennese classics, from Mozart and Haydn through Bruckner, including nearly all of the Beethoven works; second, the Mahler symphonies, for which Bernstein was so well known as a result of his CBS cycle; and third, Bernstein as a composer, with nearly all of his works, including the first recording of him conducting his own *West Side Story*. I had to convince Bernstein that penetrating the market with such a substantial volume of recordings would not be possible if he were not exclusive. He followed my reasoning but was hesitant about being tied down. In December 1979, however, with the presentation of *Beethoven Symphonies for the New Decade* in Hamburg's Vier Jahreszeiten Hotel, he was won over and the exclusivity was sealed.

Did historical considerations make it difficult for Bernstein to sign with Deutsche Grammophon?

Like most Americans, Bernstein had European roots. He was not oblivious to the atrocities during the twelve years of the Nazi regime and was most certainly not complacent about them. But he was also a man with a broad perspective and knew about Germany both before and after those times. He also knew of my Jewish-Polish roots on my mother's side and knew that there were many other Jews in the company. Whether this made his decision any easier, I cannot say.

How were his relations with the Deutsche Grammophon management?

Bernstein knew that Deutsche Grammophon meant reliability. Accuracy, discipline, punctual release dates, and perfect pressings, all signs of "German thoroughness," which in turn contributed to a special color of the recording timbre, along with the newly found German liberalism, were all factors for him.

My boss Hans Hirsch—"very German," according to Bernstein—impressed him as notably straightforward, trustworthy, and sensitive. And Hans Weber—his austere, ironical, almost omniscient recording supervisor—enjoyed Bernstein's full trust and sincere affection.

Would you say there is a "Bernstein sound?"

Over time, Bernstein's sound changed. He became less impetuous, more contemplative, and more honed. And his tempi became more drawn out. He remained very sensual, in contrast to the more analytical, intellectual approach of some of his colleagues. He became very involved not only with the score, but also with the circumstances surrounding it. Before recording the Brahms symphonies, he read the correspondence between the composer and Clara Schumann. Prior to recording *La Bohème*, he learned about life in Paris in the mid-nineteenth century. He was the most educated person I have ever met, and all of his knowledge went into his performance of a work.

How is Leonard Bernstein remembered at Deutsche Grammophon?

Bernstein commanded respect from all those who worked for him or with him. He radiated warmth and authority. People even liked his shortcomings. He had wit and curiosity in abundance. But he also knew doubt and melancholy. Nobody was indifferent toward Bernstein, nor was he indifferent toward anyone or anything. He was very political, and he engaged many politicians in exchanges of ideas. I strongly believe that even if he had never had his music, he would have been a prominent person. There is no other interpreter about whom I could say that.

How do you remember him?

Dealing with Bernstein was never easy, but always instructive and rewarding. Our relationship was characterized by sincere affection, but as his producer, I often had to talk him into making some recordings that he did not want to make and to talk him out of others that he wanted to make but which could not be taken on within the framework of a corporate enterprise.

What do you think was his major contribution to Deutsche Grammophon?

I believe that his role as a composer makes him stand out from the rest of the company's long list of stellar conductors. And the fact that we recorded his compositions so extensively makes Deutsche Grammophon stand out in his career as a very special company.

How did he work with the orchestra during studio or live recordings?

Bernstein was a marvelous teacher. He understood how to win musicians over, with patience, but also, if necessary, with firmness. He told them much about the context of a work or the drama within. The first time he conducted Mahler with the Berlin Philharmonic, he was almost driven to desperation. But by the end he was very enthusiastic. So was the orchestra. And so was the audience. Bernstein preferred live recordings because the presence of the public inspired him. It meant much more for him to play for people than for microphones.

What does Deutsche Grammophon represent to you?

I have much for which to be thankful to Deutsche Grammophon. Many of the same traits that Bernstein saw in Deutsche Grammophon were ones that I can confirm in looking back. It was a unique confluence of talents, which enabled us to save a unique perspective of this unique musician for posterity.

MAKING MAGIC
BY CRAIG URQUHART

Vice President, Public Relations and Promotion, The Leonard Bernstein Office, Inc. Craig Urquhart was assistant to Leonard Bernstein in the Maestro's last years.

Leonard Bernstein and Deutsche Grammophon—now, that's a magical combination. Then add such orchestras as the Vienna Philharmonic, Royal Concertgebouw Orchestra, Israel Philharmonic, New York Philharmonic, Bavarian Radio Symphony, and The Santa Cecilia Orchestra, and such soloists as Christa Ludwig, Thomas Hampson, Krystian Zimerman, Mischa Maisky, Gidon Kremer, just to name a few, and what a magical mix indeed! But Bernstein's Deutsche Grammophon family extended far beyond the orchestral and performing "stars"; it also included the team behind the scenes that realized the technically brilliant historic documents of the great concerts and operas that he conducted in the later years of his life.

When signing with Deutsche Grammophon in the mid-1970s, Bernstein required something no other conductor had ever asked for: that all his recordings be made from live concerts, not in the studio. The company's acceptance of this requirement is a testament to the forward thinking of Deutsche Grammophon. This new approach presented the Deutsche Grammophon recording team with a whole new set of challenges, which they met with the utmost competence.

Bernstein thought of the Deutsche Grammophon team, from the highest executive to the receptionist who answered the phone, as part of his creative-support system. However, it was his producers and recording team that he relied on the most. He trusted that their skills would translate into a recorded document as close as possible to his creative imagination. Because of this closeness, the Deutsche Grammophon team really did become part of Bernstein's inner circle. Bernstein often recorded with the New York Philharmonic in late November. So on many occasions, the team would be invited to attend Thanksgiving Day Parade parties at the maestro's New York apartment. And when on the road, the team was often invited to after-concert dinners. Lenny was the recipient not only of their combined professionalism but also of their friendship.

The friendships that were forged back then were so strong that they continue even today, even though Lenny is no longer with us. I, myself, as Bernstein's assistant in the last years of his life, had the good fortune to come to know many members of the Deutsche Grammophon team. Today, I have the privilege of remaining in touch with many of them. We often see each other, drawn together by memories of great musical events, but also by remembering the many private moments of being with Bernstein. In particular, we talk about the playback sessions, which could last for hours, as we all worked from the live performances to realize Bernstein's vision. And then, after those long hours of demanding work, the maestro would sit with us all and share a drink and a joke or two. Even today, new friendships are forming between the Leonard Bernstein Office, Inc., and Deutsche Grammophon as projects are conceived and presented to the public to continue his legacy. It is Deutsche Grammophon's dedication to music as a whole and to Bernstein in particular that make such projects possible—projects such as complete DVD releases of the Mahler symphonies; the Beethoven symphonies and overtures; the symphonies of Brahms with the Vienna Philharmonic; and the great choral works recorded with the Bavarian Radio Symphony Orchestra and Chorus. Bernstein was particularly gratified that Deutsche Grammophon took such care when he recorded his own compositions with great orchestras and soloists. What joy he would feel today knowing that a new generation of Deutsche Grammophon artists is discovering and recording his music.

Much effort by all parties went into making the recordings successful, and the demands of live recording were intense—yet there were those rare moments when it all came together without a hitch. I remember, as if it were yesterday, when Bernstein was conducting the Concertgebouw Orchestra in Schubert's Symphony no. 5. As we all sat and listened in the recording room, the team and I realized at the end of the performance that no retakes were needed—except for the last bars, which were interrupted by early applause. The audience could not contain the excitement of hearing such beauty. Magic, indeed!

[26]

[27]

[26]...[28] The gaze of an artist? Vladimir Horowitz (1903–1989), whose particular touch and imaginativeness as a performer remained intact until the end. The legendary Russian-born pianist was signed late in life by Deutsche Grammophon, with whom he traced a path that, while certainly representative of his wide repertoire, was also open to byways. His meeting with Carlo Maria Giulini, in celebration of Mozart, was one of these very successful moments.

[28]

[29]

[30]

[31]

[32]

[29] Anne Sofie von Otter has distinguished herself in virtually every field to which her brilliant mezzo-soprano voice is suited: opera, oratorio, secular and sacred music, and, of course, song. She remains one of the most cosmopolitan artists of Deutsche Grammophon's catalogue.

[30]…[32] Chamber music among colleagues of long standing (the Emerson Quartet); among friends who meet regularly (Kremer, Argerich, and Maïsky); and even within the family (the Hagen Quartet, where only the second violinist, Rainer Schmidt, is not a Hagen): three possible combinations, each producing an artistic result of the highest quality.

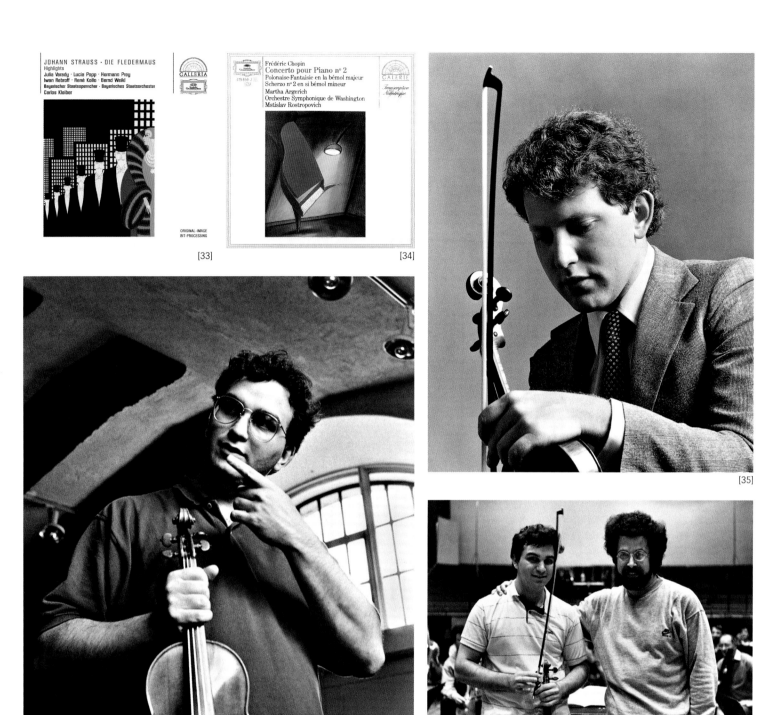

[33]   [34]

[35]

[36]   [37]

[33] [34] The mid-price series *Galleria* recycled a portion of the Deutsche Grammophon catalogue. Excerpts of operas were made available in this series, which allowed numerous classical music enthusiasts to set up a record collection cheaply while at the same time discovering the Yellow Label's famous artists.

[35]…[37] Two young violinists, Shlomo Mintz (born in 1957) and Gil Shaham (born in 1971), made an impression at Deutsche Grammophon in the 1980s and 1990s. Both have an admirable freshness and sense of style, although, as musicians, they are very different. Shaham recorded Mendelssohn's Violin Concerto with Sinopoli (shown) and Mintz Beethoven's Violin Concerto with the same conductor.

Indeed, the musical direction of the Yellow Label was still displaying an unfailing intuition. After Günther Breest (1983–1988), the direction of artists fell to Aman Pedersen (1988–1992), Roger Wright (1992–1997), Michael Fine (1997–1999), Martin Engstroem (1999–2003), Bogdan Roščić (2003–2006), Matthew Cosgrove (2006–2007), then Michael Lang (2007–). Contracts were signed with cellist Mischa Maisky (a strong personality who brought out diverging opinions) in 1982; singers Kathleen Battle (1984) and Anne Sofie von Otter (1985), and the Hagen Quartet (1985) and the Emerson String Quartet (1987); both these virtuoso quartets had styles that differed from that of the legendary Amadeus. Moreover, the Emerson Quartet had recently celebrated twenty years of continuity with no changes of members. Of the singers engaged by Deutsche Grammophon at that time, Anne Sofie von Otter is the one whose career has spanned the widest repertoire today, from lieder to oratorio, and from Baroque opera to twentieth-century music. Neeme Järvi (an enthusiast of rare repertoires) and his Gothenburg Symphony Orchestra were likewise integrated into the Deutsche Grammophon team in 1985, the same year that the Orpheus Chamber Orchestra of New York, the virtuoso "Mozart Ensemble" that plays without a conductor, was also recruited: this coincidence acknowledged the fact that orchestral music, considered as a genre, was diversifying and specializing, following the example of early-music ensembles. To celebrate the 300th anniversary of the composer's birth, Archiv relaunched an extended version of its monumental *Bach Edition* (1985).

In 1986 Deutsche Grammophon and Archiv recorded the best results of their history; the CD had, without a doubt, provided a new momentum, and already represented 62 percent of PolyGram Classics' annual turnover. The same year, Deutsche Grammophon launched its mid-priced *Galleria* series—the last to be republished (and remastered) in record format—identified by the reproductions of contemporary paintings on the record covers. But vinyl had had its day: from 1987 the series moved to CD. In another important initiative, Polydor International GmbH signed a contract with Unitel Film- und Fernseh- Produktion in Munich granting it the license to publish classic films and videos on CD Video (laser disc)—through Decca, Deutsche Grammophon, and Philips. Two very different violinists Shlomo Mintz and Gil Shaham joined the label: in chamber ensembles or with orchestra (with Abbado, Levine, Sinopoli, and André Previn), they, in turn, embarked on individual, very successful artistic journeys—proof that Deutsche Grammophon hadn't wagered everything on Anne-Sophie Mutter, although, even today, she stands apart.

THE TWILIGHT OF THE GODS

Deutsche Grammophon celebrated Herbert von Karajan's 80th birthday in 1988 in two ways: it reissued the 78s that had been recorded between 1938 and 1943, to which the conductor gave his belated approval—such a retrospective was hardly in his nature—and it released a series of twenty-five CDs, with covers illustrated with paintings by his wife, Eliette. This look back to the past was illustrated in other ways elsewhere: Deutsche Grammophon reclaimed the name Deutsche Grammophon Gesellschaft GmbH, while the *Twentieth Century Classics* series (based on the old *Collectors* series that had appeared on records) used a distinctive design to bring together modern and contemporary works of all styles and origins, including Ives, Schoenberg, Stravinsky, Webern, Hindemith, Piston, and Maderna. The pianist Maria João Pires joined the label, and she continues to establish her own personal world, one where Mozart, Beethoven, Schumann, Schubert, and Chopin are gods.

[38]

[38] [39] As a young teenager, Anne-Sophie Mutter was promoted by none other than Herbert von Karajan. Since then she has become one of the greatest violinists of our time, building a discography of incredible richness and diversity. Her position is unequalled, even today.

[39]

[40] … [44] Was it an omen? Does it remain symbolic? Herbert von Karajan, the incarnation of the musical omnipotence of West Berlin, died a few months before the collapse of the Berlin Wall, which fell in November 1989. His so-called rival, Leonard Bernstein, took the chance to celebrate this latter event with a performance of Beethoven's Symphony no. 9 that brought together musicians from the east and west. In Schiller's "Ode to Joy," he had replaced the word *freude* ("joy") with the word *freiheit* ("freedom"), symbolic nuances that his friends Claudio Abbado and James Levine would perhaps not have rejected in those days that shook the world.

[41]

[40]

[42]

[43]

[44]

[45]

[46]

[47]

[45]…[47] Pierre Boulez did not sign an exclusive contract with Deutsche Grammophon until 1991, but he had already cut some records, including *Parsifal*, recorded live at the Festspielhaus in Bayreuth in 1970, and this rare Stravinsky disc (LP 2531 377, recorded in 1980). Since then, in addition to his own works, he has made notable recordings of Debussy, Ravel, Messiaen, Bartók, Stravinsky, and the Second Viennese School. But at the heart of his legacy is, perhaps, the brilliant, complete Mahler symphonies, which Deutsche Grammophon tenaciously managed to extract from him—Boulez does not hide his preference for Symphony no. 6, with which, in fact, he began his cycle. More unexpectedly, he also recorded Richard Strauss's *Also sprach Zarathustra* and Bruckner's Symphony no. 8.

[48]

[48] [49] Plácido Domingo (born in 1941) has been the chosen partner of virtually all the great conductors involved with Deutsche Grammophon. To celebrate the 50th birthday of the great Spanish tenor, the label gave him twenty CDs for the *Domingo Edition*. Don José in Bizet's *Carmen* has been one of his favorite roles; he recorded it for the Yellow Label with Claudio Abbado, with Teresa Berganza (born in 1935 and, like Domingo, from Madrid) playing the indomitable cigarette girl.

[49]

[50]

[50] [51] After Wilhelm Kempff died in 1991 (he had already retired), Deutsche Grammophon placed their hopes on many different pianists, including the sensitive Portuguese Maria João Pires (born in 1944).

[51]

But time did not stand still: following Jochum's death in 1987, Karajan and Bernstein died only a little over a year apart from each other, in 1989 and 1990 respectively. Their last recordings were released posthumously. Strangely, Bruckner and the Vienna Philharmonic—the Symphony no. 7 for the Austrian, no. 9 for the American—brought them together for a moment.

The handing down of the baton was spectacular. First, Pierre Boulez signed a recording contract that led him to revisit, over the years, not only Mahler but also twentieth-century composers close to his heart (Stravinsky, Bartók, Debussy, Ravel, the Second Viennese School, Ligeti and, of course, his own works). Second, John Eliot Gardiner recorded his first CDs for Archiv with the Orchestre Révolutionnaire et Romantique, the ensemble that he founded to perform nineteenth-century works played on instruments of the period. Placed side by side, these two developments reveal a new perception of modernity, based, moreover, on the technological progress made by the teams at Hanover. The Recording Center developed "High-Bit" technology for two-track recording and made digital sound recordings using the "stage-box" process, which used amplifiers and converters located at the actual recording site; this technology was extended from 1991 to multi-track recordings, which gave rise to the "4-D Audio-Recording" process developed by Klaus Hiemann and Stefan Shibata that came into general use in 1993.

NEW HORIZONS, NEW ARTISTS

Wilhelm Kempff died in 1991, as did Serkin, Arrau, and then Helmut Walcha. It was the time for huge collections, which, for the most part, included some twenty–twenty-five CDs: Bernstein (1990); Domingo (1991, drawn from numerous recitals and complete collections recorded since the mid-1970s); Karajan (first, in 1990, *The World of the Symphony according to Karajan*, in eight boxed sets from Haydn to Bruckner, reissued and extended in 2008 for his centenary; then the splendid *Karajan Gold* collection, completely remastered using "Original-Image Bit-Processing," in 1993); Böhm (an admirable tribute of Strauss operas, recorded in the studio for Deutsche Grammophon, or taken from performances given in Salzburg, 1994); Ferenc Fricsay (ten magnificent CDs, including some previously unreleased recordings, 1994); Hans Werner Henze (his complete legacy from the 1960s, 1996); and, more recently, Pollini (2001). The collection celebrating the 150th anniversary of the Vienna Philharmonic, which included tapes from the Austrian Radio archives, was a huge success (1992). Was this frenzy of editions marking the beginnings of a comforting return to the past, albeit recent, a sign of the more uncertain policies of recent years? Deutsche Grammophon's history was a glorious one: the most important masterpieces had been recorded, repetition was inevitable, and the company dynamics were doubtless not the same as they had been in the past, in spite of the commercial success of the CD.

Notable conductors signed with Deutsche Grammophon from 1990 and 1995, including Myung-Whun Chung (who offered Deutsche Grammophon his first recording of Messiaen's *Turangalîla* Symphony, made with the composer's endorsement—a furrow that the Korean conductor has continued to plough steadily until today), Oliver Knussen and André Previn (also excellent composers), Christian Thielemann (notably recording Beethoven's Symphony nos. 5 and 7, which, thanks to the extended playing time, could be contained on a single CD), and Mikhail Pletnev (as a conductor first, and only later as a unique pianist, which is what he is above all). But the ambitious policies carried out by director of Archiv Produktion Peter Czornyj from 1992 concealed the underlying issues: in parallel with

[52]

[54]

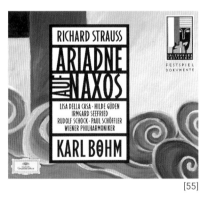

[53]

[55]

[56]

[57]

[52]…[54] Along with Karlheinz Stockhausen and Mauricio Kagel, German Hans Werner Henze (born in 1926) was a true "house" composer for Deutsche Grammophon during the 1960s and 1970s. He has recorded some of his own works from that time, in particular his symphonies.

[55]…[57] Böhm did not live to see the official release of the sumptuous *Ariadne auf Naxos*, which he had presented at the Salzburg Festival in 1954 (along with *Der Rosenkavalier*, 1969, and *Die Schweigsame Frau*, 1959). This was an intelligent use of the archives, as was the release of the famous *Rosenkavalier,* with which Karajan inaugurated the Neues Festspielhaus at Salzburg in 1960.

[58]

[59]

[60]

[61]

[58]…[61] Illuminations of the beyond . . . but also of the heart of the creative process, when a true bond is formed between performer and composer. Such was the fruit of the collaborations between Myung-Whun Chung and Olivier Messiaen, Anne-Sophie Mutter and André Previn (at that time her partner—his Violin Concerto was tailored for her like an haute-couture gown), or even Toru Takemitsu (1930–1996) and Olivier Knussen (born in 1952)—like Previn, the latter moved with ease from composing to conducting.

[62] Russian pianist and conductor Mikhail Pletnev did not need much illumination to bring his light to bear in his performance of the eighteen piano pieces by Tchaikovsky that he recorded live for Deutsche Grammophon in Zurich in 2004. As per Pletnev's own words, "I love everything about them. Whether one loves music or a woman, then one loves everything about him. Tchaikovsky remains Tchaikovsky. If I did not believe this, I would be unable to play him."

[63] [64] German conductor Christian Thielemann (born in 1959) has established himself in the traditional Germanic repertoire: Beethoven, Schumann, Brahms, Wagner, Bruckner, and Strauss, but also Schoenberg and Orff.

[62]

[63]

[64]

[65]

[66]

[67]

[65]…[67] John Eliot Gardiner (born in 1943) has accomplished an impressive tour de force: he has made his presence felt in the cantatas and Passions of J. S. Bach, Mozart's operas, and Beethoven's symphonies. His musical appetite and stylistic ease have contributed to creating the profile of a new type of conductor.

his Bach and Mozart series (the operas, from *Idomeneo* to *La clemenza di Tito* 1990–1996), Gardiner made a deep impression with his 1994 release of Beethoven's symphonies performed by the Orchestre Révolutionnaire et Romantique. Roger Norrington (EMI) and Nikolaus Harnoncourt (Teldec) had, of course, preceded him on this philological track. But this pushing back of boundaries was typical of a company for whom Karajan and the Berlin Philharmonic had made three emblematic and complete recordings of Beethoven's symphonies.

NEARING THE CENTENARY

But Czornyj was not going to stop there; he hired the very English Paul McCreesh and his Gabrieli Consort & Players, and the very French Marc Minkowski and his Musiciens du Louvre. They brought a new vision, even compared with the unforgettable accomplishments of Goebel, Pinnock, and Gardiner, to whom they were indebted. Their recordings of Italian and German choral and opera repertoire, including, for McCreesh, Handel (including *Theodora*, *Saul*, and *Messiah*) and Rameau, and for Minkowski, Handel (including *Ariodante* and *Giulio Cesare*) and Gluck, were epochal. The wind ensemble Piffaro and the sophisticated vocal groups Pomerium and the Orlando Consort were, thus, in good company. In 1993 bass-baritone Bryn Terfel, who had appeared in Strauss's *Salome* (Sinopoli) and Prokofiev's *The Fiery Angel* (Järvi), signed his first long term contract with Deutsche Grammophon. The following year, Mahler's *Symphony of a Thousand*, recorded by Abbado, saw the first use of 24-bit multitrack recording, the ultimate evolution of the "4-D Audio-Recording" process. In addition to many notable recordings of Mahler over the years, Abbado released the complete Beethoven symphonies (1999–2000) with the Berlin Philharmonic, which differ markedly from his earlier Vienna set. In the meantime, Norrington, Harnoncourt, Gardiner, and the critical edition of Beethoven symphonies edited by Jonathan del Mar and published by Bärenreiter had arrived on the scene and began to challenge accepted ideas.

Digital series made their appearance with the mid-priced *Masters*. The highlight of 1995, arguably more important even than Boulez's 70th birthday, was the launch of the *Originals* series, heir to the remarkable *Dokumente* series—the first Deutsche Grammophon *Historical* series released on CD. Reproduction of the original album covers, remastered sound, edifying notes on the performances and recording sessions: the editorial workmanship was exceptionally meticulous. It set in motion the methodical and large-scale exploration of the catalogue. Rediscoveries were numerous—many recordings had been unavailable for some time—and success was immediate: more than 2,000,000 CDs were sold in 1997. The sumptuous collection of forty-four CDs released for Fischer-Dieskau's 70th birthday brought together the landmark recordings made by the singer (Schubert, Schumann, Brahms, Liszt, and Richard Strauss), in partnership with his accompanists: Gerald Moore, of course, but also Barenboim, Wolfgang Sawallisch, and Christoph Eschenbach, the latter three also, or even primarily (in Sawallisch's case), conductors.

The new recording center built at Hanover, Emile Berliner Haus, conceived by its director Klaus Hiemann, was inaugurated in June 1996: optimal acoustic environments, cutting-edge architectural design, and the latest in recording technology were combined to create a place of excellence that is also home to PolyGram's sound archives and Mastering Center. The inauguration was linked with the *Codex* series, which brought

[68]

[69]

HANDEL
THEODORA
GABRIELI CONSORT & PLAYERS
PAUL McCREESH

ARCHIV
PRODUKTION

[70]

[68]…[71] After Goebel, Pinnock, and Gardiner, it was the turn of Englishman Paul McCreesh (born in 1960) and Frenchman Marc Minkowski (born in 1962) to contribute to the enhancement of the classical and Baroque repertoire. Their styles are as different as is possible—McCreesh's British and urbane; Minkowski's French and frenetic—though in truth, these simple labels conceal a much-more-subtle reality.

[71]

[72] Welsh bass-baritone Bryn Terfel (born in 1965) could have been a rugby player: he has the right build and physical energy. Equally at home with a popular Welsh tune or in a great Wagnerian scene, he possesses the distinctive personality and generosity that mark the greatest singers.

[73]...[75] Over the years, Claudio Abbado has become a guiding figure, an evolution that is completely natural for one who, in 1989, took up the mantle of Karajan as the head of the Berlin Philharmonic, a challenge that he met with panache and elegance, while clearly distinguishing himself both in Beethoven and Mahler.

[72]

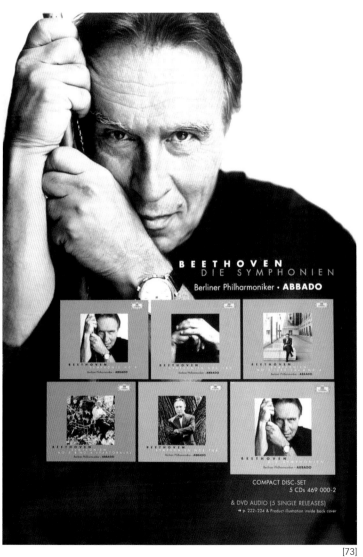

[74]

[73]

[75]

[76]

[77]

[78]

[79]

[80]

[76]…[79] Launched in 1995, the *Originals* series was an immediate success. This retrospective revealed the huge richness of Deutsche Grammophon's postwar catalogue: though Charles Munch left only Berlioz's Requiem on the Yellow Label, and the aristocratic Nathan Milstein recorded only a handful of discs (including the immortal and complete Sonatas and Partitas for solo violin by J. S. Bach), the brilliant Emil Gilels left a more substantial legacy, including this anthology of Grieg's *Lyric Pieces* as well as almost all of Beethoven's piano sonatas, completion of which was sadly interrupted by his death.

[80] [81] Dietrich Fischer-Dieskau's 75th birthday celebrations brought a renewed focus on his vast repertoire of lieder. (Here, he is seen during a recording session with Daniel Barenboim, one of his faithful associates.) There remained much to be discovered—not just rediscovered—in the sumptuous *Fischer-Dieskau Edition*—for example, the lieder composed by Wilhelm Kempff and Bruno Walter.

[81]

together treasures from the Archiv Produktion catalogue, for the label's 50th anniversary in 1997. Biber's *Missa salisburgensis* was performed at Bremen, reuniting the ensembles of Goebel and McCreesh, and the year also witnessed the release of the second *Beethoven Edition*. For this edition, historic recordings were combined with recent ones, assembling the cream of Deutsche Grammophon and Archiv's artists spanning nearly seventy years of their history. Deutsche Grammophon also announced the monumental *Centenary Collection* (ten CDs from the period from 1898 to 1945, then one per year until 1997), which was meticulously remastered using the "Virtual Gramophone" technology developed by the Emile Berliner Studios.

ONE HUNDRED YEARS OLD . . . AND MORE

By 1998 Deutsche Grammophon had a presence in more than forty countries worldwide; its catalogue contained more than 10,000 titles, of which more than 2,000 were still available (the losses were inevitable due to advances in technology and media). Eighty new recordings and 200 reissues were being released every year. Significantly, sales of Karajan recordings topped 100,000,000. This favorable state of affairs did not provide protection against industrial reorganizations, which happened more frequently in this now-global economy. Seagram's takeover of PolyGram gave rise in 1998 to the Universal Music Group. Having become the largest music company in the world, it was not long before the Universal Music Group, in turn, was acquired by the Vivendi conglomerate. In 2001 Michael Lang became general manager of Deutsche Grammophon, prior to becoming president. Sales strategies adapted to the rapidly changing buying patterns of a public for whom the Internet (and its resources) had become a daily companion.

The revival that Lang wanted resulted in exclusive contracts. With the help of media coverage and marketing, special emphasis was placed on performers, and particularly on singers, who were the easiest to promote to pop-star status. Anna Netrebko (2002), Rolando Villazón (2005), Measha Brueggergosman, Elīna Garanča, René Pape (2006), Patricia Petibon (2008), and Ildebrando D'Arcangelo (2009) thus joined the ranks of Deutsche Grammophon, which sometimes reaped the fruits of artistic talent that had begun its development under other skies: Villazón and Roberto Alagna, for example, had made names for themselves with Virgin and EMI respectively. An unexpected Handel album from Villazón, and homages to Luis Mariano and to his Sicilian roots from Alagna, did not go unquestioned—the frenzied hunt for commercial success, the desire for access to a new audience, and communication and marketing strategies inspired by the worlds of pop and rock increasingly interfered with purely artistic matters. But Terfel, Magdalena Kožená, and Thomas Quasthoff pursued or embarked upon a genuine development of the core repertoire using thematic recitals; the market no longer demanded complete operas, despite a *Traviata* (2005) and a *Bohème* (2007) that united Netrebko and Villazón, or, at Archiv, the interesting series of Handel's operas undertaken by Alan Curtis and Il Complesso Barroco. Meanwhile, in 2003, the raw 1963 version of Beethoven's symphonies by Karajan and the Berlin Philharmonic was, of course, the first historical recording to benefit from the new "Super Audio CD" (SACD) technology.

[82]

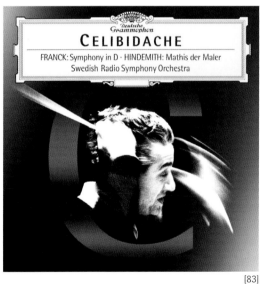

CELIBIDACHE
FRANCK: Symphony in D · HINDEMITH: Mathis der Maler
Swedish Radio Symphony Orchestra

[83]

[84]

[82]…[84] The release of a series of recordings of concerts given by the Romanian conductor Sergiu Celibidache (1912–1996) was a path that could only have been followed after his death: Karajan's unhappy rival as Wilhelm Furtwängler's successor at the head of the Berlin Philharmonic, Celibidache never officially recorded for Deutsche Grammophon, having decided very early on that recording was the sworn enemy of music and musicians. What would he have thought of these recordings being reclaimed, even with the authorization of his family?

[85]

wing on wing esa-pekka salonen
finnish radio symphony orchestra

[86]

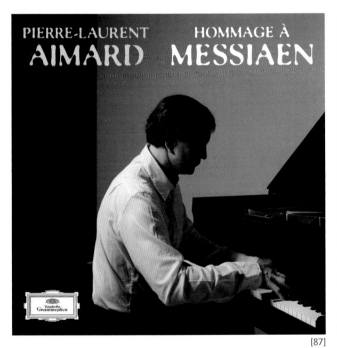

PIERRE-LAURENT AIMARD · HOMMAGE À MESSIAEN

[87]

[88]

[85]…[88] Conductors Esa-Pekka Salonen (born in 1958) and Gustavo Dudamel (born in 1981), violinist Hilary Hahn (born in 1979), and pianist Pierre-Laurent Aimard (born in 1957) are among those artists chosen today to perpetuate and revitalize the Deutsche Grammophon flame. They may not have the opportunities that their elders had of building the catalogue for the long term, but their strong and unique personalities inspire complete confidence.

On the conductor's side, other gods had become silent: Kleiber, Sinopoli, and Giulini had left the stage. Abbado, in turn, became a patron figure, albeit now more rarely, of the label (like Kubelik, Bernstein, Sinopoli, and more recently Boulez, he completed a recording of Mahler's symphonies; but following Sinopoli's example, he did not finish the Bruckner set he undertook with the Vienna Philharmonic—his compatriot had chosen the Dresden Staatskapelle). A more unexpected detour was the issuing, from 1999 to 2002, of recordings of concerts that had been given by Sergiu Celibidache in Stuttgart and Stockholm. Their release was posthumous, because the conductor had a real antipathy to recording; but Deutsche Grammophon accorded them the editorial attention and publicity worthy of Karajan, whom Sergiu Celibidache held up to public ridicule! What would Karajan himself have thought of it?

But Deutsche Grammophon also brought within its fold Esa-Pekka Salonen (his first CD, recorded in 2004, comprised of three of his works, *Foreign Bodies*, *Wing on Wing*, and *Insomnia*: like Boulez, Sinopoli, and Knussen, he is also a composer), Andrea Marcon (with Archiv, 2003) and Daniel Harding (Mahler's Symphony no. 10, 2008)—all of whom had previously worked with other companies. And Deutsche Grammophon has great hopes for the young Venezuelan prodigy Gustavo Dudamel and his Simón Bolívar Youth Orchestra of Venezuela: taking one's first steps on the Yellow Label with Beethoven's Symphony nos. 5 and 7, as has been seen, is highly significant! The most extraordinarily talented conductor to have recently appeared on the international stage, he brought with him a unique spirit and imaginativeness.

Solo performers were not neglected: not only did Deutsche Grammophon successfully manage the unexpected alliance of Argerich and Pletnev on a two-piano disc (2003), but also pianists Yundi Li (2001), Hélène Grimaud (2002), Pierre-Laurent Aimard (2007), and Yuja Wang (2008) yielded to the siren call of the Yellow Label. But it was, without a doubt, another Chinese pianist Lang Lang (2003) whom Deutsche Grammophon pampered the most, with a view to gaining access little by little to a huge market. Violinists as diverse as Hilary Hahn, Giuliano Carmignola (a dazzling Vivaldian recorded by Archiv), Vadim Repin, and Daniel Hope also joined the label between 2002 and 2007.

All things considered, this methodical and scrupulous strategy seemed reminiscent of that of big European football clubs, who sign players to prevent someone else from doing so. But, in fact, the revival was subject to these artists' playing their instruments to perfection. Inspired by the success of the *Originals*, Deutsche Grammophon launched, in parallel, the *Original Masters* series, under the direction of Alan Newcombe and David Butchart: the resultant, often imposing, anthologies rediscovered treasures, contained in the archives, from the 1950s to the 1970s. Who would have bet ten years earlier on the viability of boxed sets, devoted—to give just a few examples— to pianists Monique Haas, Stefan Askenase, or Carl Seemann (who had a wide-ranging repertoire with Deutsche Grammophon during the 1950s), or to the violinist Wolfgang Schneiderhan, or to the Janáček Quartet, or to the recordings of Paul Hindemith with the Berlin Philharmonic? Yet, though these collections were too-long absent, they stand proof to the unimpaired topicality and consistency of the catalogue built up during those years, and give a radical perspective on what followed, including Karajan.

[89]

[89] Musical talent, star quality, and commercial potential: Chinese pianist Lang Lang (born in 1982) fulfills all of these criteria.

[90] The smile of Hélène Grimaud (born in 1969) and her unique personality—both as an artist and as a woman—lend themselves to Deutsche Grammophon's declared commitment to giving pride of place to the performer.

[91] Abbado was a late convert to the use of early instruments to record Mozart. Significantly, these violin concertos with Italian violinist Giuliano Carmignola (born in 1951) were his first recording for Archiv Produktion.

[92] A typical cover from the *Al fresco* series launched by Archiv, adorned with drawings by the French painter Henri Matisse.

[90]

[91]

[92]

[93]

[94]

[95]

[93] French tenor Roberto Alagna (born in 1963) is on a mission to win the hearts of the masses. After a trip to Mexico to promote his disc devoted to the operetta singer Luis Mariano, he takes us to his parents' native Sicily.

[94] Rolando Villazón (born in 1972) in a recording session, as expressive and committed as when on stage—a side of him that the general public does not get to see.

[95] Russian singer Anna Netrebko (born in 1971), posing like a supermodel or film star. The boundaries between classical music and show business are being erased, and the images of artists are now more and more controlled.

[96]

[97]

[98]

[96]…[98] The German bass René Pape (born 1964), the Latvian mezzo-soprano Elina Garanca (born 1976), and the German bass-baritone Thomas Quasthoff (born 1959) are three of the key singers currently successful with Deutsche Grammophon.

[99]

[101]

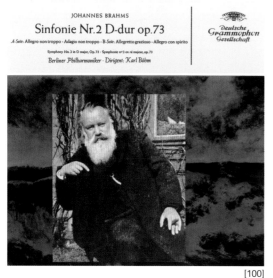

[100]

[102]

DG WEB SHOP

[103]

[99] ... [101] In parallel with developing a strategy adapted to the current dominance of the media, Deutsche Grammophon has explored its past with extraordinary relevance. This has given rise to important series, such as *Original Masters* and *Musik . . . Sprache der Welt*, the latter reusing the visuals from the original records, as seen here in a recording of Brahms's Symphony no. 2, conducted by Böhm. The photograph shows Austrian violinist Wolfgang Schneiderhan (1915–2002), who recorded an extensive discography in the 1950s.

[102] [103] Is this the future, or just one opportunity in uncertain and changeable times? Many concerts given by Deutsche Grammophon artists are now downloadable from the Internet, by way of DG Concerts. Only time will tell if this new, virtually infinite,arena will be capable of generating a new audience, and thereby new markets, for classical music.

This trend expanded into many vintage series that were meticulously remastered: *Musik . . . Sprache der Welt* (2004) for recordings from the 1950s, which were presented in their original sleeves (with the yellow band either centered vertically or horizontally across the top), and *Master Recordings*, a collection of Karajan's work (2007). The Archiv reissues were more limited (the *Blue* collection and, particularly, *Al fresco*, for its 60th anniversary). Fischer-Dieskau had again been honored in 2000, on the occasion of his 75th birthday: ranging from 1949 to 1981, the twenty CDs in this collection explore the unique range of his recorded repertoire (including the reissue of his recording of Reimann's opera *Lear*, in a role that he created in Munich in 1978). It was also necessary to systematically transfer the Unitel collection onto DVD, an undertaking that today is virtually complete, and this has been wisely sustained by new productions (for example, *La Traviata* and *Manon* with Netrebko and Villazón, and Gounod's *Roméo et Juliette* with Nino Machaidze and Villazón). However, it was a joint project with Decca, the release of recordings of all of Mozart's operas, performed together for the first time at the 2006 Salzburg Festival in celebration of the 250th anniversary of the composer's birth (Mozart 22), that was seen as the year's most significant event.

AND NOW?

Is the disc dead, as prophets of doom (they have always existed) have been declaring for a long time already? Artistic policy is no longer what it was; nor is the market as congested; and the potential audience can easily get lost in today's overabundance of recordings of the classical repertoire that has always shown itself to be the heart of Deutsche Grammophon's activities. With its offices now situated in an historic building near the port of Hamburg, the illustrious Hanseatic label has understood that it cannot limit its future activities to the CD. Exploration of the infinite possibilities offered by the Internet has been an obvious way forward: since 2006, DG Concerts have introduced Internet users to the world of concerts given in Los Angeles, London, or New York—almost immediately (within a few months, or even a few weeks)—thereby also avoiding the prohibitive costs incurred by even the shortest studio session as soon as many people need to be involved. Direct sales of the whole of the catalogue currently available began in 2007 via the DG Web Shop, which now also provides downloads of more than 1,000 recordings that are missing from the "normal" catalogue. Will that be enough? It is probably too soon to say. But in making these changes, Deutsche Grammophon has demonstrated, once again, its ability to connect with the evolution of a new era. It is, therefore, not unreasonable to look forward to the next chapters of its splendid history with optimism. Isn't yellow, after all, the color of the sun?

BILL HOLLAND
Former Managing Director, Universal Classics and Jazz UK

You were the managing director of Universal Classics and Jazz UK from 1983 to 1990 and returned in 1996 as Universal Classics and Jazz Managing Director until your semiretirement at the end of 2006. How would you describe Deutsche Grammophon in a few words?
The Rolls-Royce of classical record labels. Deutsche Grammophon is synonymous with the highest ideals of artistry, technical quality, creativity, and brand marketing, which has positioned the label as superior to its competitors and the best that money can buy.

What makes Deutsche Grammophon unique?
The widespread, traditional view that the Deutsche Grammophon label has a reputation second to none has been lodged in consumers' psyche for many years. In my view, Deutsche Grammophon's exalted position was achieved by the following simple and uncompromising strategy: (i) Signing exclusive contracts with and investing in the greatest musicians in the world (singers, instrumentalists, orchestras, and conductors). (ii) Engaging the most talented and creative A&R, marketing and promotional professionals to work closely with the artists and their management teams. This spirit of close cooperation resulted in a commitment to share the highest artistic ideals and maximize the sales potential of the records. (iii) A close relationship with the print and broadcast media, developed and nurtured by the Deutsche Grammophon promotional team, which enhanced the profile of the label. Deutsche Grammophon surpassed other companies by establishing a competitive advantage. This manifested itself in trips for key journalists to the international music festivals and regular business lunches to brief the media on forthcoming plans. (iv) A creative design team for CD booklets, publicity material, and advertising far advanced in comparison with what other labels had to offer. Stylishness was paramount, and the style always highlighted the core values of the label.

What was the image of Deutsche Grammophon in the second half of the twentieth century?
From the advent of the LP record through to the advent of the CD, Deutsche Grammophon was considered to be peerless in the quality of its LP pressings and state-of-the-art sound quality. Classical-record buyers were totally convinced that, in all aspects, Deutsche Grammophon had a product (super-shiny-black vinyl) that not only looked vastly superior to its competitors' LPs, but even had a protective inner sleeve that was itself a thing of beauty. In those early days, the Deutsche Grammophon sound was particularly admired and cherished by both consumers and the media alike. When the CD was launched in the early 1980s, Deutsche Grammophon was especially proactive in putting the silver disc on the map. With Herbert von Karajan as a principal advocate of the medium of CD, the Deutsche Grammophon label was perceived as being at the forefront of the new technology.

When did Deutsche Grammophon really start to be perceived as an international label, rather than as a German/Austrian one?
In the United Kingdom, there was a real sense that Deutsche Grammophon was a "German import" label well into the 1960s, but not in any negative sense. It was highly respected and valued by collectors. Even now, in 2009, there is a perception that it is a great German label that happens to record international artists. The evolution from Deutsche Grammophon's being considered German/ Austrian is so gradual as not to be time specific.

Unlike Furtwängler, who used to compare LPs with "cans," Deutsche Grammophon has always been very interested in technological progress. How did the CD launch influence Deutsche Grammophon's image?
The launch of the CD in the United Kingdom stirred up a debate about the merits, or otherwise, of CDs, when compared to LPs, and Deutsche Grammophon was at the center of this debate. I vividly recall the occasion of Karajan presenting the CD to the media in Salzburg in 1981. He was greatly interested in technological change: "All else is gaslight," he proclaimed after hearing a CD playback. In reality, Deutsche Grammophon, Decca, and Philips CDs were manufactured in the same factory, but some media that did not support the medium of CD chose to specifically criticize Karajan recordings, citing compression of sound, narrow dynamic range, and unnatural highlighting and balancing of instruments. This negative press may well have been connected to Karajan's proselytizing of the CD. However, sales were phenomenal, with many collectors replacing their worn LPs and swelling the numbers of new-release sales.

In 1983, the repertoire centers (Decca in London, Philips Classics in Baarn, and Deutsche Grammophon in Hamburg) combined under a single management (PolyGram Classics International). What changed for Deutsche Grammophon?
Fears that the three PolyGram Classics labels would become one proved unfounded. The three labels were intensely competitive with each other, as well as with the opposition, and label identity remained a priority. Certainly, some costs could be saved by sharing certain resources, but in many ways, Deutsche Grammophon enjoyed some of its greatest artistic and commercial successes after the merger of the three PolyGram labels.

How would you describe the global evolution of the classical music industry and how did Deutsche Grammophon react?
It became clear, as the CD market matured and plateaued, that countless versions of the same repertoire could not be financially justified. Of course, conductors want to record, for posterity, their interpretations of Beethoven, Brahms, Tchaikovsky, Mahler, et al, not only once, but sometimes two, three, four, or more times. Painful decisions had to be made. With many companies' having remastered and restored their back catalogues, an abundance of fine recordings was available at competitive prices. Naxos launched its range at a budget price, and many consumers were happy to purchase their desired works performed by unknown artists. Deutsche Grammophon reacted rightly, in my view, by not competing head on, but by continuing to focus on its great artists, to make great records, and to offer, as it always had, a range of less-expensive reissues drawn from its back catalogue. However it was becoming clear that there were turbulent times ahead for the whole industry, and, like all companies, Deutsche Grammophon viewed each potential new recording as something that should be justified, both artistically and commercially.

Would you say that classical music in general, and Deutsche Grammophon in particular, has a wider audience today than twenty years ago?
Fewer records (CDs) are being sold today than twenty years ago. There is more piracy and home copying. However, both live and recorded music has a potentially larger worldwide audience than ever before. Accessing that audience is the challenge, not only for record companies, but also for concert promoters, teachers, musicians, colleges, and anyone else who believes that music is fundamental to civilized existence.

[01]

FIFTY YEARS OF STEREO IN THE SERVICE OF MUSIC

THIERRY SOVEAUX

Although the advent of the microgroove or LP in the early 1950s laid the foundations for modern high fidelity (thanks to a much broader bandwidth than that of the 78 rpm), it was stereophonic sound that would bring in the real revolution: henceforth, sound as a fixed point, almost abstract and lacking in spatialization, gave way to a two-dimensional sound image. With it came an impression of relief, an ability to place the various instruments or voices in the virtual space, and of greater musical clarity, creating the credible impression of a live performance.

It was in 1957 that Deutsche Grammophon decided to jump on the stereo bandwagon, recording the great repertoire for posterity in the best technical conditions possible in order to create a complete phonographic museum. This was the equivalent in sound of the famous work *Museum Without Walls*, which had been written a few years earlier by André Malraux, and was finally benefiting from color, under the direction of publishers Albert Skira and Gallimard.

The first stereophonic discs recorded by Deutsche Grammophon appeared in 1958. The ephemeral 136 000 stereo series, released at the same time as the monophonic 18 000s current at the time, began with Richard Strauss's *Also Sprach Zarathustra*, recorded in Berlin with Karl Böhm on the podium. But it was Eugen Jochum who inaugurated the famous 138 000 series, which would continue until 1968, with Schubert's Symphony no. 9, recorded in Munich. Meanwhile, the brilliant young Lorin Maazel recorded Stravinsky's *Firebird*, and Igor Markevitch the suite from Rimsky-Korsakov's *Coq d'or*, albeit on a 25cm (10-inch) disc (133 000), a less expensive series that was abandoned in 1962.

The more popular format of mono discs (18 000) still represented the majority of releases: Rita Streich with immortal songs; Maazel's first Beethoven with the Berlin Philharmonic; Dietrich Fischer-Dieskau with Otmar Schoeck's lieder; Imgard Seefried with a Schubert recital; Jochum at the beginning of his complete Bruckner with Symphony no. 5; not to mention pianists Géza Anda, Jörg Demus, and Sviatoslav Richter, who were released simultaneously in mono and stereo. The first two-channel recordings, made with few microphones, as was customary at the time, favored clarity, limpidity (*The Firebird* and *The Pines of Rome* with Maazel), and naturalness. The sound is distinguished by an almost insistent clarity, especially for voices. Unlike American (RCA and Mercury) or British (Decca) rivals, there was a refusal to take the "sound spectacular" route. In short, Deutsche Grammophon's postwar roster of artists, assembled by the highly talented Elsa Schiller, took flight with recordings, which, on artistic and technical levels, remain to the present day some of the most beautiful in the catalogue.

FRICSAY AND JOCHUM: THE PIONEERS

At the end of the 1950s, Ferenc Fricsay undertook what was to have been a complete recording of the Beethoven symphonies with the Berlin Philharmonic, but it was sadly cut short by his untimely death in 1963. The recordings of Symphony nos. 3, 7, and 9 remain models and marvelously translate the specific sound of the Berlin Philharmonic of that era, with a real density in the strings and a rawness in the woodwind and brass, not yet possessing the polish and sophistication of the later Karajan versions. The sound image is perfectly limpid, but this time demonstrating the orchestra's volume and natural substance. Dvořák's famous *New World* Symphony, perhaps the finest in the discography, meets these same criteria.

At the time, Fricsay was recording numerous discs with his RIAS-Symphonie-Orchester, and two discs embody almost miraculously the Hungarian maestro's aesthetic, which combined precision, clarity, and expression to the exclusion of post-Romantic indulgence or excess. There were the marvelous opera ballets recorded in 1959: never has the suite from Gounod's *Faust* sparkled with such elegance, refinement, and quality of articulation. An absolute respect for timbres—that great Deutsche Grammophon quality—is on display in the marvellous Bartók/Stravinsky/von Einem disc: the suite from Kodály's *Háry János* avoids ostentation in favor of integrity and continual appropriateness of color.

As for Eugen Jochum, after a superlative set of Brahms symphonies with the Berlin Philharmonic—but in mono—he undertook the complete Beethoven symphonies: the considerable closeness of the musicians, the flexibility of texture, the transparency of the different sections, and the naturalness of timbres produced a realistic sound for the late 1950s that won widespread acclaim. Jochum's career would be punctuated with major recording successes, including, in addition to his famous Bruckner, Mahler's *Das Lied von der Erde* with the Amsterdam Concertgebouw and the collaboration with Heinz Wildhagen, who would later be called upon for Rafael Kubelik's Mahler cycle, discussed below. There were also the two Brahms piano concertos with Gilels in the early 1970s which, thanks to the microphones of Klaus Scheibe, revealed a more biting Berlin Philharmonic, perhaps with more presence than usual, and also Haydn's *London* symphonies, beautifully recorded with the London Philharmonic for *The World of the Symphony*.

[02]

[03]

[01] The cover of a promotional leaflet released at the time of Deutsche Grammophon's transition to stereo in 1958.

[02] Lorin Maazel at the end of the 1950s.

[03] SLP 133 006, recorded in June 1958 at the Salle Pleyel in Paris. This record from the 133 000 series is 25 cm (10 inches) in diameter.

[04] Ferenc Fricsay in rehearsal with the RIAS-Symphonie-Orchester.

[05] SLPM 138 828, recorded in 1960/61 in Berlin.

[06] SLPM 138 038, recorded in October 1958 at the Jesus-Christus-Kirche in Berlin. This performance of Beethoven's Symphony no. 3 by the Berlin Philharmonic is one of the most beautiful since that of Furtwängler.

[07] SLPM 136 211, recorded in 1961 at the Jesus-Christus-Kirche in Berlin: Fricsay conducting at his peak, with clarity, articulation, and an absence of sentimentality.

[08] SLPM 138 127, recorded in October 1959 at the Jesus-Christus-Kirche in Berlin.

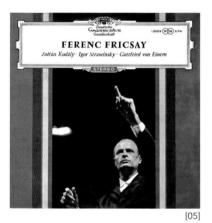

[05]

[06]

[07]

[08]

[04]

[09] SLPM 138 037. Beethoven's Symphony no. 1 was recorded in April 1959 with the Bavarian Radio Symphony Orchestra at the Herkulessaal in Munich, and no. 8 with the Berlin Philharmonic in May 1958 at the Jesus-Christus-Kirche in Berlin.

[10] SLPM 138 865, recorded in March/April 1963 with the Amsterdam Concertgebouw Orchestra. This performance of Gustav Mahler's *Das Lied von der Erde* ("The Song of the Earth") is, without a doubt, one of the most authentic recorded over the last fifty years on any label.

[11] CD 447 4462. A beautiful rerelease in the *Originals* series of LP 2707 064, first released in 1972.

[10]

[09]   [11]

[12] SLPM 138 657, recorded in London in November 1960. An outstanding recording by Harald Baudis of a legendary performance.
[13] Jochum in rehearsal with the Amsterdam Concertgebouw Orchestra, of which he was principal conductor from 1961 until 1964. Amsterdam was a stronghold of the Mahler cult.

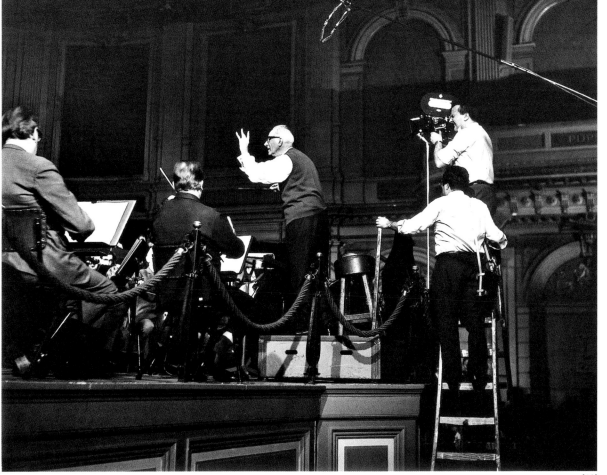

[12]   [13]

The 1960s opened with a magnificent set of Tchaikovsky's last three symphonies by Mravinsky and the Leningrad Philharmonic Orchestra, recorded in London during a tour. While the interpretation defies all comparison, the technical quality of these recordings is among the finest ever realized by the German firm in any era: the dynamics and the placing of the different sections in a three-dimensional, stereophonic space are close to ideal, thanks to Harald Baudis, who would be responsible for some of the catalogue's finest recordings.

Meanwhile, Karl Böhm continued his Strauss recordings in Dresden with *Der Rosenkavalier*, then *Elektra*. His contribution to the Austro-German repertoire in the second half of the twentieth century would be among the most definitive, alongside that of his alter ego and compatriot Herbert von Karajan.

THE BÖHM SOUND FROM CONCERT TO DISC

While Karl Böhm made his first records for the Yellow Label during the war years, the Austrian conductor's major achievements coincided with the firm's golden age. At the end of the 1950s and during the 1960s, the conductor made most of his recordings with the Berlin Philharmonic, as "his" orchestra, the Vienna Philharmonic, remained under exclusive contract to Decca. At the beginning of the 1970s, a new contract finally tied the Viennese orchestra to the Yellow Label, an event inaugurated by a recording of Beethoven's Symphony no. 5, with Böhm conducting, of course. This disc caused a sensation for the quality of the interpretation as well as for the recording itself, as the orchestra was finally heard in its own hall, the Musikverein. It had left the famous Sofiensaal, where all of the great Decca recordings were made and which had not survived a recent fire, for the natural setting of the Musikverein. This unique orchestra had at last rediscovered its true colors, without lapsing into the spectacular. In concert, Karl Böhm's sound image was characterized by tremendous stability in terms of sound and music in the balance between the strings, never complacent, the woodwind, always easily distinguishable, and the truly majestic brass. The impression of air, of breathing that ran through the sections, was gripping, this sound aesthetic a style probably acquired through Mozart. Indeed, the operas of the Salzburg master were conceived as gigantic wind machines: the woodwind sound like human voices; human voices sound like oboes, bassoons, or clarinets.

From this point of view, the live 1974 recording of Mozart's *Così Fan Tutte*, from Salzburg, is highly informative: the microphones of Günter Hermanns, Karajan's recording engineer, succeeded miraculously in capturing the ethereal lightness and incomparable elegance. Already in his recording of the complete Mozart symphonies, made in Berlin during the 1960s, Böhm was beginning what he considered the business of his life: restoring to favor an authentic Mozart style based, in particular, on rebalancing winds and strings in a more discreet way than in the post-Romantic tradition; to be convinced of this, it is necessary only to listen again to the *Prague* Symphony (Originals). On the other hand, Böhm nurtured a true passion for his beloved Vienna Philharmonic; the near-magical expanded space that runs throughout the whole orchestra is particularly noticeable in the *Pastoral* Symphony of 1971 (*Originals*), an extraordinary Bruckner Symphony no. 7 or, yet again, in Strauss's *Heldenleben* of the same year. Moreover, these faithful recordings perfectly respect the conductor's musical wishes.

[14]

[15]

[16]

[18]

[17]

[14] Karl Böhm rehearsing Beethoven's Symphony no. 9 with the Vienna Philharmonic in April 1970.

[15] SLPM 138 113, recorded in October 1959 at the Jesus-Christus-Kirche in Berlin.

[16] LP 2530 781, recorded in Vienna in 1976.

[17] LP 2709 068, produced in 1976.

[18] SLPM 138 018, recorded in April 1958 at the Jesus-Christus-Kirche in Berlin.

HERBERT VON KARAJAN: A UNIQUE SOUND

Herbert von Karajan's name is inseparable from the Yellow Label. *Semper et ubique*, the maestrissimo was accustomed throughout his career to signing simultaneous "exclusive" contracts (with Decca, EMI, Deutsche Grammophon, of course, and Sony for Home Video). But it was to Deutsche Grammophon that he granted the lion's share, with nearly 400 recordings.

The Austrian conductor's first recording for Deutsche Grammophon goes back to the war years—1938 to be exact—with the overture to *The Magic Flute*, which would be followed by some twenty-odd more, spread over five years. After the war, Karajan joined the EMI group and Walter Legge, in London, for about ten years. At the end of the 1950s, he signed a new contract with the German firm, under the direction of Elsa Schiller and inaugurated by the famous, emblematic Strauss *Ein Heldenleben*. The heroic, demonstrative sounds explored the potential of the newborn stereo to its fullest, even accepting the famous left-right effect that Deutsche Grammophon had largely shunned. However, with this recording, which has become legendary, the technical and artistic team that would contribute so much to the elaboration of the Karajan myth was not yet formed, and the famous "Karajan–Deutsche Grammophon sound," still constantly evolving, was not entirely distinctive from that produced by the EMI or Decca teams, which were also current in the late 1950s.

THE WONDERFUL DECADE

It was the celebrated 1962 Beethoven cycle that would seal, for at least ten years, a sound aesthetic that became mythical. Recorded in the Jesus-Christus-Kirche in Berlin-Dahlem, these discs, the first stereo set of Beethoven's complete symphonies in history, would set a new standard in terms of quality as well as distribution. Although Elsa Schiller was still in charge of the set's production, it was Günter Hermanns who would henceforth be in charge of all of the maestro's recordings, with very few exceptions, until Karajan's death in 1989. Curiously, the sound of these recordings achieves a strange alchemy between technology and the sound and musical aesthetic demanded by Karajan. To this is added the blossoming of a new-style Berlin Philharmonic displaying clear improvement: peerless soloists, sound generated with, until then, unknown refinement, the revelation of the famous "Stromlinie" or "aerodynamic" sound—liquid and ethereal, elegant and sensual—that was meant to smooth over any harshness, the whole combined with the famous *tenuto*, moving from attack to extinction without weakening.

Otto Ernst Wohlert, then Otto Gerdes, would succeed Elsa Schiller in the course of the glorious 1960s, but Günter Hermanns would remain at the console, capable of capturing like no one else that iridescent beauty, recognizable anywhere. The Brahms symphonies followed Beethoven, before Tchaikovsky, and above all, the memorable Sibelius recordings, the stuff of legend. Then there were Bruckner's Symphony no. 9, Haydn's *Creation*, Wagner's *Der Ring des Nibelungen*, and Prokofiev's Symphony no. 5, a great, perhaps incomparable, harvest in the midst of Karajan's plethoric discography.

However, this fairly characteristic style, which some would describe as "without conflict" and "beyond human," displayed an Apollonian style that did not always correspond to the reality of concert performances, which were more committed, feverish, and sometimes passionate almost to excess. All these elements recall the uniqueness of the Deutsche Grammophon sound in those glorious years.

Deutsche Grammophon invented compatible mastering in the early 1960s to make mono and stereo cartridges compatible. Until then, a mono disc could be read only by a mono cartridge, and a stereo disc only by a stereo cartridge. The producers were then able to issue the same recording in mono or stereo, the latter being the more expensive version.

KONZERT FÜR MILLIONEN

Deutsche Grammophon thus decided to simplify the process and reduce production costs in exchange for certain compromises: the bandwidth remained in mono, resulting in channel separation and a dynamic range inferior to those of true stereo discs. As proof, it is enough to compare a Deutsche Grammophon LP recorded in the 1960s with a Decca disc. In an article accompanying a promotional disc put out in the 1960s, producer Otto Ernst Wohlert tried to gloss over the limitations of this process by justifying an aesthetic and pointing out the constraints of modern life: one could not hope to reproduce the 100 or 120 dB of the Berlin Philharmonic at home without getting into a row with one's neighbors! Limiting the dynamic range of a recording and its playback to 70 dB meant that the "nuisance" caused—added to street noise—was between 30 and 50 dB. In that halcyon era, dominated by the miracle of German economic growth, Deutsche Grammophon principally targeted cultured, city-dwelling executives, dominated by an essentially Anglo-Saxon civic-mindedness. Certainly, these widely distributed LPs—thanks to Karajan, boasting exemplary and faithful reproduction of timbres—did not fully succeed in reproducing the fullness and volume of a symphony orchestra; the compression is noticeable in the *fortes* or *fortissimos*, and the low register lacks some solidity; the accuracy of color and instrumental contours, combined with a somewhat cramped sound image, are quite characteristic of the Deutsche Grammophon sound in the 1960s and 1970s.

Nonetheless, if one compares Karajan's Deutsche Grammophon recordings from the late 1960s or early 1970s with the EMI recordings produced following the new contract signed in 1969, the advantage would remain with Hamburg's integrity. Although Michel Glotz and the EMI recording engineer Wolfgang Gülich managed, it is true, to reproduce the sweep of the Berlin Philharmonic in all its depth (Beethoven's Triple Concerto and Mozart symphonies), overall, the sound image seems artificial, characterized by a lack of precision on the instrumental contours and timbres that are insufficiently dense. Indeed, the major producers of the period—EMI, Decca, RCA, CBS (American Columbia), Philips, and Deutsche Grammophon— had strong identities that could be easily distinguished by the passionate audiophile. Everything contributed to this, from the often-powerful personality of the artistic director and that of the recording engineer to the manufacturing of the physical disc, pressing, and quality of the resin—and this was all to the advantage of a company with its own spirit and formulas. Deutsche Grammophon's high-quality pressing resulted in discs that were particularly silent in soft musical passages: surface noise was imperceptible, unlike French, English, or American records of the time—a very real asset.

[19]

[20]

[21]

[22]

[19] Karajan in rehearsal for the recordings of Brahms's symphonies with the Berlin Philharmonic in 1964 at the Jesus-Christus-Kirche in Berlin.

[20] CD 477 7157 from the Karajan *Master Recordings* series.

[21] SLPM 138 025, recorded in March 1959 at the Jesus-Christus-Kirche in Berlin. This was an historic recording for the Deutsche Grammophon label: the first postwar stereo recording made by the Austrian conductor. The rest is history.

[22] Karajan conducting the Berlin Philharmonic in 1963.

[23]

[24]

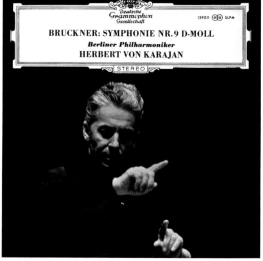

[25]

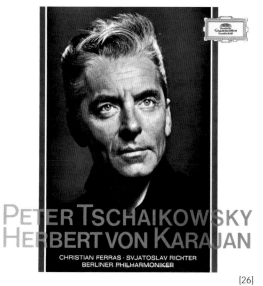

[26]

[27]

[28]

[23] A test recording in September 1962 of Beethoven's Symphony no. 9 with the Berlin Philharmonic at the Salzburg Festspielhaus. The actual recording was made in November 1962 at the Jesus-Christus-Kirche in Berlin with the same orchestra, chorus, and soloists.

[24] SLPM 139 282, recorded between 1966 and 1968. This is, without a doubt, one of the greatest versions of Haydn's *Creation*. The Austrian tenor Werner Krenn took over from Fritz Wunderlich, who died in 1966.

[25] SLPM 139 011, recorded in 1966 at the Jesus-Christus-Kirche in Berlin.

[26] The boxed set of the complete Tchaikovsky, which was released on subscription in 1967.

[27] The rerelease in the *Originals* series of the 1968 recording (SLPM 139 040) surpasses the original in terms of both dynamics and bandwidth.

[28] A live performance, recorded and filmed, of Beethoven's Symphony no. 9 by the Berlin Philharmonic in 1968.

[29] An overhead shot of the Berlin Philharmonic during filming for Unitel in 1967.

[29]

In the 1970s Karajan pursued his feverish quest for quality. The introduction of the Dolby system, which reduces tape hiss while, alas, suppressing the natural rawness of the recording, was added to the mix of a multi-microphone setup in view of future plans for quadraphonic sound, which would end in failure. The sound image of these discs is a long way from the realism of the concert hall, as can be heard by listening to the Strauss discs of the period (*Four Last Songs* with Gundula Janowitz, *Death and Transfiguration*, and *Also Sprach Zarathustra*). If we compare Karajan's second stereophonic cycle of the Beethoven symphonies with the first, the advantage goes incontestably to the earlier version, which is both more natural and more faithful.

In 1979, following a highly convincing listening session in the Sony studios, the maestro demanded that his recordings should henceforth be digital. This would be the case with Mozart's *The Magic Flute* and Strauss's *Alpine* Symphony. The former, initially released on vinyl in 1980, does not avoid a disappointing harshness of timbres, a hazard endemic to this new technology; on the other hand, the *Alpine* Symphony boasts appealing limpidity, plasticity and impressive dynamics. *Parsifal*, recorded the following year at great expense, leaves hardly anything to be desired in terms of dynamic and frequency range or spatial definition.

The splendor of the Karajan/Berlin sound was at last perceptible and continued in 1982 with Mahler's Symphony no. 9, which was recorded live by Günter Hermanns. The incomparable Bruckner Symphony no. 8 of 1988, performed by the Vienna Philharmonic, remains the greatest testimony to Karajan's later work for its artistic as well as its technical quality, offering astounding dynamics and a faithful reproduction of the Philharmonic's colors.

KARAJAN FOREVER

Karajan's finest discs thus span three decades of recording for the Yellow Label, and recent remastering gives some of them a splendor that the LP did not always achieve. In addition, they attest to the excellent quality of the original sound recordings, finally freed from the limitations mentioned above, in particular those owing to compatible mastering. The Beethoven Symphony nos. 3 and 4 of 1962, remastered by the Emile Berliner Studios (*Master Recordings*, 2008), surpass all earlier editions and attain the very highest standard.

Similarly, the Berlin Philharmonic's harmonious beauty and natural phrasing are on magnificent display in the rerelease of Brahms's Symphony nos. 2 and 3 of 1964 (*Master Recordings*). The Sibelius symphonies (1965–1967) show Karajan at his best, nos. 4 and 5 being some of the finest sound recordings achieved by Günter Hermanns. As for the remastering of the Ring (*Originals*), it would even give the Solti/Vienna Philharmonic version, tremendous on vinyl but disappointing on CD, a run for its money. Haydn's *Creation* also reveals a hitherto-unknown freshness, whereas Prokofiev's Symphony no. 5 (1968) lavishly reproduces the splendor of the Berlin Philharmonic at its height (Originals). These discs, produced by Otto Ernst Wohlert, then by Otto Gerdes, preserve a particular mood.

The 1970s would be dominated by the famous boxed set devoted to the Vienna School (1973–1974), recorded with the greatest care. In Schoenberg's Variations for Orchestra, for example, Karajan demanded that certain instruments be separated by Plexiglas partitions to bring out

[30] Herbert von Karajan in 1971 talks to the recording team during a recording session.

[31] The remastered rerelease of Brahms's Symphony nos. 2 and 3 in the 2008 *Karajan* collection.

[32] LP 2530 368 recorded in 1974.

[33] Karajan's last recording on CD in 1988, Bruckner's Symphony no. 8. This was not the end, however: Bruckner's Symphony no. 7, recorded at his last concert in April 1989, was released after his death).

[30]

[31]

[32]

[33]

MICHEL GLOTZ
Herbert von Karajan's Executive Producer

You were Herbert von Karajan's friend from 1957 until his death in 1989 and his producer at Deutsche Grammophon from 1974. You were, therefore, a privileged witness of the collaboration between the label and the conductor. What was this relationship like?

The relationship between them was a very friendly one, notably because of the respect and affection that Herbert von Karajan had for Günther Breest. He also got on very well with Pali Meller Marcovicz and the technical team. I think that their collaboration was at its best during the latter part of his life. It had begun in 1959, when Deutsche Grammophon was about to lose Ferenc Fricsay. It was then that Elsa Schiller felt the need to approach Karajan because she was looking for another renowned conductor. He didn't call upon my services until a lot later, however—at the time his contract was being renewed in 1974, when he was recording Bach's Mass in B Minor. But I had already worked with him for a long time at EMI.

When I arrived, I received a lovely welcome from Deutsche Grammophon's technical team, in particular, from Herbert von Karajan's sound engineer, Günter Hermanns. The directors were at first more reserved, which I understood completely, because I had spent most of my career with EMI, and it was a bit difficult for them to integrate a man coming in from the outside. But that resolved itself quite quickly. And my collaboration with Deutsche Grammophon lasted until March 1989, three months before Karajan's death.

Would you agree that there was a "Karajan sound?"

There was; it's undeniable, but Günter Hermanns, too, was no stranger to it. It was, above all, rich, full, sensual. Contrary to what has often been written, the sound was reworked relatively little technologically, except at times—to bring out the strings, at others the brass—in accordance with Karajan's wishes. But we never manipulated the sound to enhance a legato or alter the volume. As for sound montages, we made them, of course, but we never exaggerated the sound. Our main concern was to preserve the music exactly as it had been recorded, so that the recording conformed in every respect to what Karajan could have re-created in a concert.

Having followed Herbert for more than thirty years, I'm well placed to comment on the fact that this idea of a "Karajan sound" has been overdone; it's as though we were talking about a recipe or fixed form. For this sound evolved, not only, of course, in accordance with his own aesthetic research, but also because of the technological developments made in sound recording and media, which, we often forget, determine the final sound reproduction. That doesn't mean, however, that there was no aesthetic coherence, but this was living, evolving, if I can say that. And not only did Karajan adapt perfectly to technological change in order to make the best aesthetic use of it, but he also constantly researched new developments. This is the reason why he rerecorded the main works in his repertoire, such as the symphonies of Brahms and Beethoven, many times.

His aesthetic vision, as has often been written, was Apollonian: it consisted of producing the most voluptuous sound, by making the music as beautiful as possible, as opposed to raw music, where we would have disregarded all of the technical details that determine the final result. From the point of view of pure aesthetics, Furtwängler, Walter, and Toscanini were his models. He was a synthesis of Germanic discipline and Mediterranean creativity. He often made a point of saying that he was an Austrian with Greek roots.

Digital recording enabled this richness of the "Karajan sound" to be realized extremely accurately. Deutsche Grammophon, having very rapidly obtained two 3M recorders, in case one of them broke down, was quick to benefit from the early days of digital recording. We made a large number of discs together with this new medium. And fortunately, the remastering of his earlier analog recordings also did justice to his work and reproduced, in all its fullness, the sound of this earlier era.

What were his relationships with the label's other great orchestral conductors like?
He didn't have a lot to do with his peers, with the exception of Giulini, whom he admired enormously. There were young conductors about whom he was passionate; and, among the conductors of his own generation, Lorin Maazel, whom he liked a lot. His *répétiteur* at the piano was Christian Thielemann, who has since become the great conductor that everyone knows. Karajan was also on very good terms with Leonard Bernstein, whom he always invited to lunch when they met in Europe. He had more than mere respect for him. Bernstein, perhaps, even exerted a certain influence on Karajan, in that his passion for Mahler was quite infectious and moved Karajan. Strangely, Karajan came to this great composer only late in his life. And I wonder if it wasn't the example of Bernstein, who gave himself so generously in his performances of Mahler's symphonies, that encouraged Karajan to interpret some of these symphonies himself, particularly nos. 4, 5, 6, and 9.

KARAJAN AND I
BY EWALD MARKL

1981–1989: Recording Producer for Deutsche Grammophon and Philips in Vienna. 1989–2003: Head of the Deutsche Grammophon offices in Vienna and Deutsche Grammophon Executive Producer

The year, 1938, in which the thirty-year-old Herbert von Karajan produced his first record—Mozart's Overture to *The Magic Flute*—in Berlin, was also the year of my birth. Karajan's first recordings, involving four orchestras—the Berlin State Orchestra, the Berlin Philharmonic, the Orchestra Sinfonica della RAI di Torino, and the Amsterdam Concertgebouw Orchestra—were released by the Deutsche Grammophon label between 1938 and 1943. After the war, Karajan continued recording for EMI in Vienna and London.

I heard Karajan for the first time on October 1, 1954, at the Vienna Musikverein. This was a life-changing experience for me and marked the start of an addiction that I will touch upon later. The Vienna Symphony Orchestra's *Karajan Cycle* featured Mozart's Symphony no. 39 in E-flat Major, K. 543 and Anton Bruckner's Symphony no. 5. Tickets for this cycle were always virtually given away for just a few Austrian schillings by the Theater der Jugend, the forerunner of the Jeunesse Musicales. By way of comparison, that same year, my first LP record (Beethoven's Piano Concerto no. 5 with the Philharmonic Orchestra and soloist Walter Gieseking—a humble LP sleeve with no text or photos, the only adornment being the stickers for the A and B sides), also, of course, conducted by Karajan, cost 198 Austrian schillings. The second Karajan concert followed just one week after the first. This was *Carmen*, a concert version performed in French at the Musikverein with Simionato in the leading role and Nicolai Gedda playing the role of Don José.

If he had been allowed to do so, Karajan would have shown his growing number of Musikverein supporters what he was capable of at the Vienna Opera House (at the time known as the Theater an der Wien). However, he was banned from the Opera House because Wilhelm Furtwängler would only agree to perform in Vienna on condition that Karajan would not be allowed to perform there at the same time. This was the same Furtwängler who, just as Karajan was conducting the above-mentioned Bruckner concert, made his last appearance as conductor at the Musikverein, on the occasion of the studio recording of *The Valkyrie* with the Vienna Philharmonic. He died two months later.

Everything changed in 1956. Karl Böhm resigned from the Vienna State Opera, and in June 1956, Herbert von Karajan gave his first-ever guest performance at the Musikverein with the Berlin Philharmonic. During the third and final concert, the *Tannhäuser* Overture was played as an encore, which was interpreted by many opera fans as a foretaste of things to come. Just one week later, La Scala, Milan, gave a triumphant guest performance of *Lucia di Lammermoor* at the Vienna State Opera, with Maria Callas in the leading role. Karajan's appointment as artistic director of the Vienna State Opera swiftly followed.

However, there was nothing operatic about his first performance in his new role on January 17, 1957, at the Vienna State Opera, when Karajan dedicated Mozart's *Maurerische Trauermusik* (or, *Masonic Funeral Music*) to the memory of Arturo Toscanini. Ten weeks later, the Karajan era began with *The Valkyrie* and ended on July 17, 1964, with a performance of *Die Frau ohne Schatten*, with many great Verdi, Wagner, Puccini, and Richard Strauss evenings in between.

I have particularly fond memories of four other events: an *Oedipus Rex* performance with Jean Cocteau as narrator in 1958, then in November 1961, Herbert von Karajan in the unusual role of conductor of a ballet performance: an adaptation of Holst's *The Planets*. In 1962 I enjoyed a performance of Debussy's *Pelléas et Mélisande*. I'd managed to get myself a seat in the side stalls for this concert. I couldn't see a lot of the stage, but I had a wonderful view of the nonchalant Karajan on his rostrum as, with the slightest wave of his hand, he brought the orchestra to life. Finally, in 1963, I enjoyed Erich Kraack's revised version of Claudio Monteverdi's *L'Incoronazione di Poppea*. A few days later, Lothar Knessl gave a lecture at the Musikhaus 3/4 and played excerpts from recordings (obviously at this time without any contributions from Harnoncourt and Gardiner), explaining to the sparse audience that this version was nothing like Monteverdi's own.

In between operas, Karajan regularly returned to the Musikverein (he only ever graced the Konzerthaus with his presence once in his long career) and from 1958, at the latest, these concerts offered an additional visual attraction—long blonde hair, like Mélisande's fair locks, cascading down from the Musikverein director's box. This was Eliette von Karajan, newly wed and surrounded by honorable gentlemen who had met Johannes Brahms in person. Around this time, in March 1959, Herbert von Karajan started recording with Deutsche Grammophon again. This was a happy union that was to last until his death in 1989.

In the Recording Studio

Sometime around then, my excessive record purchases (due for the most part to the ever-growing number of Karajan new releases) began to cause an alarming deficit in my budget that I did not overcome until I entered the recording industry at a relatively late stage. In other words, in 1981 I became head of the classical section for Deutsche Grammophon and Philips. My first duty in my new role was to present Karajan's new *Falstaff* recording with Giuseppe Taddei in the leading role and the Vienna Philharmonic.

Interestingly, this recording was released on the Philips label; Deutsche Grammophon had already committed itself to producing a Giulini recording at the same time. EMI had already produced a *Falstaff* performance—the legendary Gobbi recording—conducted by Karajan, and, therefore, had no particular interest in a duplicate. So this meant that Philips received one of Deutsche Grammophon's Falstaff productions and celebrated the only Karajan performance in its catalogue, as though it had won an unexpected lottery prize. One of the privileges of my job included being allowed to attend all of Karajan's last recordings at the Vienna Musikverein, whereas all other eavesdroppers were accompanied out of the room by the conductor's bodyguards. I thus witnessed Karajan at work during his productions of *Turandot*, *Der Rosenkavalier*, and *A Masked Ball*.

During *Turandot*, he experimented by lining up the singers in front of the stage. During the *Rosenkavalier* production, Vinson Cole passed the time devouring countless novels before finally being called to deliver his aria on the last day of recordings; and during *A Masked Ball*, I was allowed to make a tape recording of the Toscanini LP overnight as Karajan wanted to listen to it the next day. Some time after the release of the *Turandot* recording, Karajan recorded the final act of the opera again during a symphony performance. Meanwhile the CD age had dawned, and Karajan, the perfectionist, wanted to take advantage of the greater dynamic facilities offered by CD technology.

Karajan always recorded in long takes, scarcely interrupted, and only ever had the manuscript in hand when making corrections with the team over the phone. I have seen conductors' scores with more annotations and comments on them than the notes themselves. Karajan's scores, which can still be seen today in his Anif and

St. Moritz homes, could be sold tomorrow as brand-new copies. The recordings themselves were always undertaken in an atmosphere of quiet concentration with never a loud word spoken. He would only become audibly irritated if interrupted during his work (but who in their right mind would do such a thing?).

Once, one of the many microphones failed during a movement of a Tchaikovsky symphony. During the recording, a Deutsche Grammophon technician crawled forward, like a soldier in a trench, in an attempt to discreetly replace the microphone. Of course, he was spotted by Karajan, who immediately stopped the musicians and yelled, "What's he doing there?" He wasn't interested in the stammering explanation and cried out, "We've got enough microphones," before indignantly starting up the orchestra again. There was another time, during a New Year's Eve concert, when a microphone went on strike. This time it was the hand microphone, which was passed to Karajan so that he could deliver his New Year's greeting. The wonderful message ("I wish peace, nothing but peace and more peace to one and all") that can be heard on the DVD actually began quite differently. The microphone cut out, and Karajan mumbled, "That's a great start to the year," before being hurriedly passed a functioning microphone, enabling him to deliver the message that we are all familiar with.

Studio recordings always followed the same ritual. After a few takes, Karajan would enter the mixing room, nod briefly, and comment with a grin, "Too loud!," before they had even started the tape rolling. Otherwise, he had no airs or graces. He had trusted his team for years—from the recording manager to the cable bearer. He had earned the image of an aloof and arrogant maestro through many years of cooperation (or rather noncooperation) with the media, but he enjoyed a remarkably good relationship with his recording managers and audio-control engineers. Men such as Weber, Garben, Glotz and, in particular, Günter Hermanns understood him just as well as the London, Berlin, and Vienna orchestras. After a passage from the second movement of Dvořák's Symphony no. 8 for a Deutsche Grammophon recording in Vienna in the winter of 1985, Karajan told the orchestra that he could only hear bar lines, and that each bar line was like a slap in the face. I believe that Herbert von Karajan could not have verbalized his musical "credo" any more precisely.

Sometimes, at the request of her husband, Eliette would make a sudden appearance in the recording studio to listen to a test cut alongside Herbert and his crew. She would not be expected to comment on anything such as balance or intonation. It was rather her intuitive opinion that was appreciated, and her affinity with Herbert's intuition was truly remarkable.

Rare Occasions: Ceremonies and Official Appearances
Even the few official ceremonies had their own recurring sequence of events, including the mandatory Gold Disc awards. If I remember rightly, back then in Austria, the award was presented for 25,000 copies sold. During the ceremonial presentation, Karajan would always ask how many copies the golden disc represented. Each time he would give the same disappointed answer, "Is that all?"

Karajan could also be heard to laugh loudly and heartily, such as one evening when enjoying a meal at the Grotta Azzura following the end of the Rosenkavalier recordings. Heinz Zednik, who had played Valzacchi during the production, parodied his singer and conductor colleagues all night. Herbert von Karajan shook with laughter and could not get enough of it. I hasten to point out that Zednik did not include Karajan in his imitations!

The Grotta Azzura had been chosen quite deliberately, as Karajan had been a regular guest there during his time at the Vienna State Opera. The landlord at the time, Libero Arbace, had even managed to get his name on the credits of one of Karajan's recordings. In May 1961, Verdi's Otello had been recorded for Decca at the Sofiensaal venue in Vienna. Tom Krause sang the small part of the herald and, due to the insignificance of his role, had asked to remain anonymous; Libero Arbace eagerly offered up his name, and it has adorned the LP and CD covers of this recording for almost fifty years.

When the aforesaid Rosenkavalier was released on the market, Karajan was asked during an interview why he had decided to bring out this new release after EMI's wonderful 1950s recording. In his reply, he hinted at the fact that he had, at last, found his Marschallin in Anna Tomowa-Sintow and (purposely, perhaps) forgot to mention that, at the time, Elisabeth Schwarzkopf had been perfect for the role. When confronted with Karajan's statement, Schwarzkopf counterattacked with comments that could hardly be described as fitting for a Marschallin.

An Inquiring Mind Right to the End

Where most conductors are concerned, the general pattern is that their repertoire diminishes with age. Not so with Karajan. His plans for the early 1990s included a third recording of Bach's Mass in B Minor, and also the first ever recording of Carl Orff's *Carmina Burana*, Gustav Mahler's Symphony no. 2, and Bellini's *Norma*.

During the 1980s, he produced new releases of all of Beethoven's and Brahms's symphonies for audio- and videocassette, along with the first-ever LP recordings of umpteen works, including a set of late Haydn symphonies, Carl Nielsen's Symphony no. 4, Jean Sibelius' *Pelléas et Mélisande*, and Richard Strauss's *Alpine Symphony*.

When not busy conducting, stage-managing, or rehearsing, he liked to slip into his colleagues' rehearsals. In this way, in 1985, he witnessed Horst Stein's rehearsal of Richard Strauss's *Capriccio* in Salzburg. This resulted, just a few months later, in Karajan's recording not the entire opera but rather the "Moonlight Music" interlude and the Countess's monologue in Berlin. While watching the rehearsal of Penderecki's *The Black Mask*, Josephine Barstow caught his eye for the very first time and was to become his Amelia in *A Masked Ball*. He began recording work with her at the beginning of 1989; however, on July 16, during rehearsals for this opera on the occasion of the Salzburg festival, Herbert von Karajan died at his Anif home.

Thus his concert on April 23, which no one could have suspected would be his last performance, was to be my final encounter with Karajan. This was a matinee concert at the Vienna Musikverein with the Vienna Philharmonic. The program exclusively featured Anton Bruckner's Symphony no. 7, with Deutsche Grammophon's taking care of the live recording. Originally, it had been intended that Schubert's *Unfinished* Symphony would be performed just before the interval, however Karajan had felt tired during rehearsals and had decided to concentrate solely on Bruckner's symphony.

A few members of the orchestra had also suffered health problems that April. As soon as the first rehearsal was over, a delegation of horn players entered the conductor's dressing room, presenting their battered lips. Karajan asked them despairingly, "What do you want me to do—heal you?" However instead of a miracle healing, horn players from the Munich Philharmonic arrived on the next plane, saving Karajan's last-ever concert and last-ever recording.

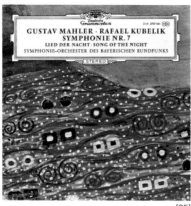

[34]…[38] Kubelik recorded the complete Mahler symphonies in Munich at the Herkulessaal toward the end of the sixties with the Bavarian Radio Symphony Orchestra. The conductor is shown here (38) with Heinz Wildhagen (seated on the left) in discussion during a Mahler recording session in 1967.

particular instrumental parts that cannot normally be heard in the concert hall. During the same period, the microphones were removed from the Jesus-Christus-Kirche and redirected to the Berlin Philharmonic, which was difficult to tame and suffering from a form of compression in the middle register. Recording techniques were also becoming more and more sophisticated.

STEREOPHONY DEMONSTRATED ON ONE COMPOSER

This was the title of an article by Heinz Wildhagen in the book *The World of the Symphony*, published in 1972 to coincide with the disc release of the same title. At the time, this recording engineer was placing the microphones for the complete Mahler symphonies by Rafael Kubelik. The conductor had, with his musical understanding, sketched out the stereophonic effects called for by the composer with regards to the sound of a large orchestra. The aim was to provide the listener with a sound image that was, from a certain point of view, better than what would be heard in concert, especially in terms of acoustic clarity.

One essential feature distinguished this Mahler cycle from all other recordings: the arrangement of the strings (the first violins at the front on the left with the double basses behind, the cellos in the middle, and the second violins at the front on the right with the violas arranged behind them). This arrangement, which Kubelik always preferred, enhanced the stereophonic effect, providing greater differentiation between the first and second violins, whose sound floated like a curtain before the orchestra.

Another example of this comes in the fifth movement of Mahler's *Resurrection* Symphony, in which the composer asked for precise acoustic effects, such as the introduction of an orchestra in the distance with trumpets and percussion instruments. The composer wrote: "It must have such a weak echo as not to infringe in any way on the nature of the sung part with cellos and bassoon; like isolated sounds of barely perceptible music, borne by the wind." The technical solution was to have an additional orchestra playing in a separate room, without any optical or acoustic connection with the hall; the same solution was used with the chimes in the last movement of Symphony no. 6.

As for the vocal parts, Heinz Wildhagen explained his way of positioning the singers within the overall sound. In Symphony nos. 2, 3, and 4, the solo parts were relayed differently, depending on their individual characters; they were partially integrated into the overall sound of the orchestra but also juxtaposed with it, so that it was possible for the same voice to be heard at different acoustic levels in the movements of the same symphony. "This was not a technical blunder," explained Wildhagen, "but a deliberate means of expression."

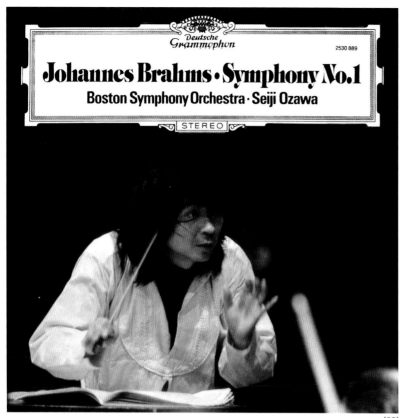

[39]

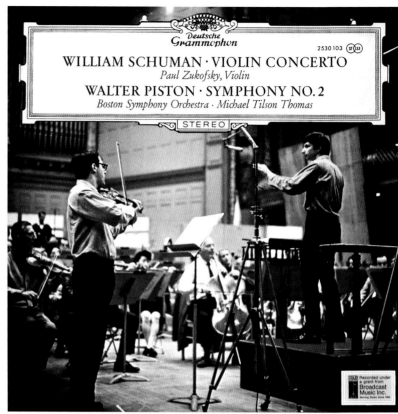

[40]

[41]

[42]

[39]…[42] LP 2530 888, recorded in 1977. LP 2530 103, recorded in 1971. LP 2530 787, recorded in 1977. LP 2530 048, recorded in 1970. During these years, Deutsche Grammophon opened itself to modern and contemporary American music, which was little known or appreciated in Europe at that time.

CONQUERING AMERICA

In 1969 the Boston Symphony Orchestra suddenly broke its long-standing contract with RCA, a partnership that had lasted several decades. At that same time, the Yellow Label was seeking to expand its sphere of activity to the United States. With the Berlin Philharmonic under Karajan, followed by the Vienna Philharmonic with Böhm and the Bavarian Radio Symphony Orchestra with Kubelik, and soon after that the London Symphony Orchestra with Abbado, the German firm had signed some of the finest European orchestras. However, it was well known that the beauty of exceptional ensembles, such as the Vienna and Berlin Philharmonic Orchestras and the Amsterdam Concertgebouw (under exclusive contract with Philips), was counterbalanced by the technical perfection of American orchestras, such as those of Chicago and Cleveland—or that of Boston, shaped by Koussevitzky, Munch, Leinsdorf, and William Steinberg. It was Claudio Abbado who celebrated the new relationship between Boston and Hamburg with a very fine Debussy/Ravel album in the autumn of 1970.

From 1971 one recording followed another, including world premieres such as *Sun-Treader* by Carl Ruggles and Walter Piston's invigorating, uncompromising Symphony no. 2, at the same time as a marvelous, dreamlike Tchaikovsky Symphony no. 1. It was a twenty-four-year-old conductor, the promising Michael Tilson Thomas, who directed those very fine Boston recordings, produced by Karl Faust; Günter Hermanns achieved a dynamic sound that perfectly reproduces the unique characteristics of Boston's Symphony Hall, famous for its remarkable acoustics. Especially from this point of view, Holst's *Planets*, conducted by William Steinberg and rereleased in the *Originals* series, remains a model. Numerous recordings were released in the following years, in particular at the instigation of Seiji Ozawa, the orchestra's music director. Memorable among these is a lovely version of Berlioz's *Roméo et Juliette*, as well as two much less well-known discs released simultaneously in 1977: Brahms's Symphony no. 1 and Tchaikovsky's Symphony no. 5, both feverish yet controlled and admirably recorded by Klaus Hiemann. During the same period, with Hans-Peter Schweigmann at the controls, Ozawa conducted a first-rate recording of Charles Ives's Symphony no. 4, which boasts astounding dynamics.

FORMULA UNO: CLAUDIO ABBADO

The winner of the Koussevitzky Competition in 1958, Claudio Abbado accepted Karajan's offer to conduct Mahler's Symphony no. 2 at Salzburg with the Vienna Philharmonic. The Italian maestro had already joined Deutsche Grammophon in 1967, recording Prokofiev's Piano Concerto no. 3 and Ravel's Concerto in G in Berlin with Martha Argerich. This disc created a sensation because of its poetry and stylishness. The partnership continued in London with a no-less-famous Chopin/Liszt disc. But committed to transalpine culture, and looking toward Vienna, where he had studied, Abbado nurtured a passion for Brahms and Mahler as well as for the musicians of the Second Viennese School. With the Berlin Philharmonic, he recorded Brahms's Serenade no. 1, followed by a top-notch Symphony no. 2 in 1970. This would be the prelude to a complete set of Brahms's symphonies, now largely forgotten, and featuring four different orchestras: the Vienna Philharmonic (no. 1), the Dresden State Orchestra (no. 3), and the London Symphony Orchestra (no. 4).

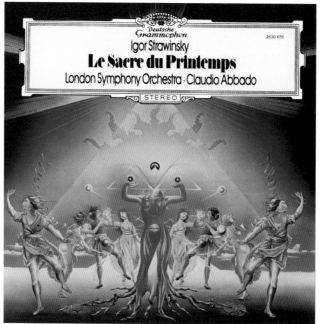

[43]

[44]

[45]

[46]

[43] Claudio Abbado at his home in Milan during the 1970s.

[44] LP 2530 635, recorded in 1976. The cover design is by Peter Wandrey.

[45] SLPM 139 371, recorded in November 1967 at the UFA-Tonstudio in Berlin. This recording was one of Abbado's first with Deutsche Grammophon.

[46] LP 2530 424, recorded in 1974 at the Musikverein in Vienna.

[47]

[48]

[47] [48] LP 2720 063, recorded in 1972: *The Barber of Seville*, with the London Symphony Orchestra, considered at the time to be one of the top operatic orchestras. Abbado knew how to maximize the orchestra's precision. Jean-Pierre Ponnelle, at the height of his career, directed and produced the film. Hermann Prey, a loyal supporter of the Salzburg Festival since 1959, played the title role with great dramatic flair but without pretentiousness.

[49]

[50]

[49] [50] *Carmen* conducted by Abbado, recorded in Edinburgh and London in 1977, in association with the Edinburgh Festival. It was Peter Diamand, the festival's director at that time, who managed to persuade Teresa Berganza to sing the title role. She agreed on condition that Piero Faggioni's production erased the image of Carmen plying her charms, which Berganza considered discourteous to Spanish women.

Although a curious, very open-minded man who acknowledged his special attraction to Viennese music, Abbado soon demonstrated his keen interest in Italian opera, and Rossini in particular. Meeting Teresa Berganza proved to be a decisive moment, and their collaboration was inaugurated by the famous *Barber of Seville*, released in 1972. What could indeed be called the renewal of Rossinian singing was followed immediately by *La Cenerentola*, which is full of grace and simplicity as well as piquancy, with a refreshing return to the original instrumentation. The celebrated and musical *Carmen* of 1977 is in the same vein and is one of the most beautiful recordings ever made by Deutsche Grammophon: dynamics, presence, limpidity, sound staging…all the winning ingredients are there.

The Rossini adventure would continue into the 1980s with the famous *Viaggio a Reims* and *L'Italiana in Algeri*, both displaying the same verve and precision. In addition, Abbado developed a real passion for Mahler, recording the complete symphonies over several years at the head of some of the world's finest orchestras: the London Symphony, Vienna Philharmonic, Chicago Symphony, and Berlin Philharmonic. Abbado also demonstrated remarkable refinement in twentieth-century repertoire: for example, in Debussy's *Pelléas et Mélisande*; in Bartók piano concertos with Pollini; in Prokofiev; in the *Wien Modern* concerts, recorded live in Vienna; and in recordings of Nono, Schoenberg, Webern, and Berg, including an outstanding *Wozzeck*, captured live at the Vienna Opera in 1987.

WOZZECK: FROM BERLIN TO VIENNA

The Böhm version, recorded in 1965 in Berlin, preceded Boulez's Paris recording by a year and followed the historic but technically limited recording by Dimitri Mitropoulos in New York (1951). This first stereophonic *Wozzeck* played the card of perfectly assumed Viennese modernity. Böhm conducted with a keen sympathy for Berg's music and with a constant concern for continuity between the past and the present: this time, the brotherly warmth of *Fidelio* and the hothouse atmosphere of *Tristan* give way to burning ice. In the original LP booklet, producer Otto Gerdes explained the aesthetic choices governing this recording: the undertaking aimed at shedding light on the score's complexity and refinements by endeavoring to transpose stage and visual effects onto the acoustic and sound levels. To do so, the studio walls were modified in order to obtain a relatively long reverberation time. In that way, the direct sounds could be captured before the return of the echo, favoring greater limpidity. The recording of this modern work strives for a certain continuity with musical classicism, and the refinement of Böhm's supremely subtle conducting is unfailingly translated by the quality of the sound. Yet there remained the impasse of dynamics, Deutsche Grammophon's shortcoming at the time.

Abbado's live recording of Berg's opera was of a completely different nature, reflecting a more expressionistic approach with greater contrast, admirably captured by Klaus Hiemann's microphones, which were placed in the pit of the Staatsoper close to the musicians. This modern recording allowed the orchestra to be captured in close to its full dynamic range. Everything is heard with ease, without the impression of a veil, and the singers' movements are perfectly "visible," creating a sound image that is practically three-dimensional. Again, the craftsmanly care brought to the Böhm version, which had, from this point of view, incomparable appeal in terms of sound and music, had, in twenty years, given way to a naturalness and clarity that left barely anything to be desired.

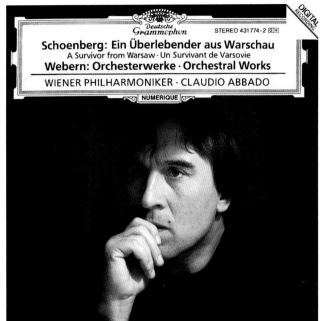

[51]

[52]

[53]

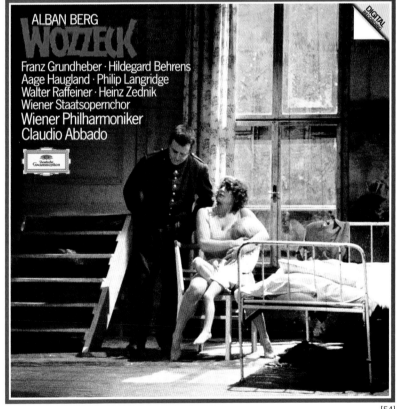

[54]

[51]…[54] Whether with the experienced Vienna Philharmonic or the Gustav Mahler Youth Orchestra, in the Second Viennese School or serial music, Abbado has always held an important place in contemporary music, both in concert and in recordings. He made the most of his position as *Generalmusikdirektor* of the Vienna State Opera (1986–1991) to convince the city's political and cultural leaders to create a contemporary music festival, and succeeded in founding the Wien Modern festival in 1988. A year earlier, also with the Vienna Philharmonic, he made an outstanding live recording of *Wozzeck* at the Vienna State Opera. Deutsche Grammophon had also recorded another memorable *Wozzeck*, this time in a studio, with Fischer-Dieskau and Evelyn Lear (SLPM 138 991/92, recorded in 1965 at the UFA-Tonstudio in Berlin).

THE AMADEUS QUARTET: THIRTY YEARS OF FIDELITY

Three of the musicians in the Amadeus Quartet (Norbert Brainin, Siegmund Nissel, and Peter Schidlof) were Austrian by birth, which explains in part the Mozartian choice of name for their ensemble. In truth, there was a more important reason: the close spiritual relationship between these musicians and the Viennese classical triumvirate: Haydn, Mozart, and Beethoven.

After emigrating to England in 1938, the three instrumentalists met the young British cellist Martin Lovett before founding the Quartet in its original form; its members would never change. The Amadeus Quartet's recording career with Deutsche Grammophon began in 1950, two years after its first concert, at the Wigmore Hall in London. Recording all of Beethoven, all of Mozart, and all of Haydn, as well as Schubert, Brahms, Smetana, and Dvořák, they would become the equivalent of Dietrich Fischer-Dieskau for the Austro-German vocal repertoire or Wilhelm Kempff for the Austro-German piano repertoire: a symbol of excellence in chamber music for three decades. The specific Amadeus sound—clear, homogeneous, powerful, and dense in certain cases but always supremely balanced—was highlighted by Deutsche Grammophon. The label's reliable technological precision faithfully reproduces the quartet's unmistakable tonal qualities.

THE REVIVAL OF GERMAN SONG WITH DIETRICH FISCHER-DIESKAU

If there was one singer who symbolized Deutsche Grammophon's quality during the latter part of the twentieth century, it was, without a doubt, Dietrich Fischer-Dieskau. This in no way diminishes the merits of Irmgard Seefried, Rita Streich, the incomparable Fritz Wunderlich (whose career was cut tragically short), Gundula Janowitz, Hermann Prey, Teresa Berganza, or, more recently, Anne Sofie von Otter and Bryn Terfel. The German baritone made his first disc in 1949, when he was only twenty-four. Like Karajan and Schwarzkopf, he built his career around the disc, seeking to record the finest music for posterity. Even though he participated in numerous opera recordings, in particular conducted by Fricsay, Böhm, Karajan, Jochum, and Keilberth—his portrayal of Barak in *Die Frau ohne Schatten* remains unforgettable—it was in song, and with the German lied in particular, that he truly distinguished himself. This new style of singing, fundamentally literary and highly attentive to the meaning of the words and the slightest vocal inflection, found its perfect medium in the intimacy of recording. Some reproached Fischer-Dieskau's singing for being overly sophisticated or even mannered, and for lacking in spontaneity and naturalness, but the sheer scope of his legacy commands admiration. It was in the recording of 600 Schubert lieder, at the turn of the 1960s, that this renewal of Schubertian singing found its highest achievement. The closeness of Hans-Peter Schweigmann's microphones brought out the minutest nuances of this brilliant singer-actor, creating an intimacy impossible to achieve in the vast space of a concert hall, while favoring the concentrated listening that only a disc can offer. The singing is perfectly balanced with the infinitely sensitive piano playing of the great Gerald Moore.

[56]

[57]

[55]

[55]…[57] The Amadeus Quartet at King's Lynn, Norfolk, in 1981. The members of the quartet, which was founded in 1948, remained the same throughout its history. The death of viola player Peter Schidlof in 1987 brought the musical and recording career of the famous quartet to an end. The other members, Norbert Brainin (first violin), Siegmund Nissel (second violin), and Martin Lovett (cello) considered Schidlof completely irreplaceable and so decided to disband.

[58] SLPM 139 219/20, recorded in July 1966. Fritz Wunderlich, who died prematurely in September 1966 at the age of thirty-five, claimed that Deutsche Grammophon was "…the company for me!" He had signed an exclusive contract with the firm in 1964 and found, there, artists that he admired and with whom he worked very productively: Herbert von Karajan, Karl Böhm, Karl Richter, Dietrich Fischer-Dieskau, Gundula Janowitz, Christa Ludwig, and many others.

[59] SLPM 136 546, recorded in 1967 in Berlin. Gundula Janowitz's pure Mozartian voice here serves the cause of a subtle and refined interpretation of Wagner.

[58]

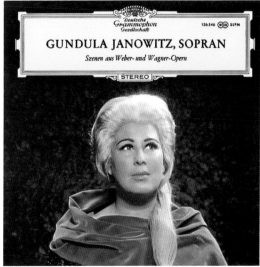

[59]

[60]

[62]

[63]

[61]

[60] Dietrich Fischer-Dieskau during a recording session.

[61] SLPM 138 911–14, recorded live in November 1963 at the National Theatre in Munich.

[62] SLPM 139 201/02, recorded in 1965 at the UFA-Tonstudio in Berlin. Fischer-Dieskau recorded Schubert's *Winterreise* with the Austrian pianist Jörg Demus. Like Moore, Demus was a great accompanist.

[63] LP 2707 097, recorded in 1976. This version of Mahler's Symphony no. 9 by Giulini was praised by critics worldwide.

[64] Giulini conducting the Vienna Philharmonic during live recordings of Brahms's symphonies.

[64]

CARLO MARIA GIULINI CONDUCTS BRAHMS, BRUCKNER, AND MAHLER

Brahms, Bruckner, and Mahler occupied a special place in Carlo Maria Giulini's musical pantheon. In the mid-1970s, the Italian conductor signed a contract with Deutsche Grammophon for a series of recordings of works particularly close to his heart. Recorded in 1977 and produced by Günther Breest with Klaus Scheibe at the console, his Mahler's Symphony no. 9 is one of the three or four most beautiful recordings in the work's entire discography, with great transparency and breathtaking dynamics that do justice to the tremendous power of the opening movement. The intense, powerful playing of the Chicago Symphony Orchestra comes close to a certain kind of perfection.

Later on, in the early 1990s, Giulini recorded the Brahms symphonies with the Vienna Philharmonic, live from the Musikverein, with rich, smooth sound evoking boundless nostalgia from an orchestra possessing sublime, golden colors. Andreas Holschneider, together with Hans Weber and Günter Hermanns, supervised the recording. Finally, a special mention must be given to the incomparable recording of Bruckner's Symphony no. 9, which even today still dominates the entire discography of the work, with its precisely reproduced timbres, the perfect stability of its miking, and its dynamics suffering from no apparent compression whatsoever.

HALF A CENTURY OF OPERA IN STEREO

Deutsche Grammophon's very first stereophonic disc, with organist Helmut Walcha, was produced in 1956. The German firm applied this technology to the world of opera beginning in 1957 with Ferenc Fricsay's recording of Beethoven's *Fidelio*. Stereophony could, at last, translate the full complexity of the skillful combination of orchestra, singers, and chorus, taking into account, when necessary, the movement of singers on a virtual stage. Fricsay, who had signed a contract with Deutsche Grammophon in 1949, then undertook the recording of Mozart's operas, begun in mono, and that would continue with *Don Giovanni* and *The Marriage of Figaro*.

Karl Böhm, as guardian of the Straussian legacy, conducted the first stereo *Rosenkavalier*. The presence of the singers in the foreground has its virtues, although there is an occasional emphatic quality in the upper frequencies; clearly, a kind of absolute limpidity was sought. Fricsay's *Don Giovanni*, *The Marriage of Figaro,* and *Fidelio* adhere to the same aesthetic, as does Weber's *Freischütz*, conducted by Jochum.

Böhm's *Elektra*, on the other hand, is of greater homogeneity and, on the level of musical clarity, even wins out over the famous Solti version, recorded in the mid-1960s for Decca. Decca has always been celebrated for its sumptuous, deliberately spectacular productions, seeking a sort of audio equivalent of CinemaScope, but not all of these lavish productions have stood the test of time. Whereas Decca tended somewhat to "drown" singers in the midst of a luxuriant, if occasionally intrusive, orchestra, the Deutsche Grammophon microphones achieved a balance between the orchestra and the singers that is ultimately more satisfying. EMI, which resisted stereophony longer, chose to overlook the movement of singers in the virtual space in favor of a serious aesthetic that favored pure musicality, the result being more like a concert.

Lisa Della Casa als Arabella und
Dietrich Fischer-Dieskau als
Mandryka in »Arabella«
Gesamtaufnahme in der Besetzung
der Münchener Opernfestspiele
in Vorbereitung

Zauberreich der Oper

Es scheint, dass sich das Wunder der modernen Schallplatte in der Opernaufnahme — der einzelnen Arie, des Querschnitts wie der Gesamtfassung — am eindrucksvollsten dokumentiert: Über die Kunst des Interpreten und die Schönheit und Natürlichkeit der modernen Aufnahmetechnik hinaus, die Zeit und Ort der künstlerischen Manifestation vergessen macht, ist die Opernschallplatte oft genug imstande, auch die Bühne, auf der das Werk doch beheimatet ist, vollauf zu ersetzen. Einzig die Musik, die schöne Melodie, die dramatische Kraft einer Gesangsszene triumphiert — durch die Macht der menschlichen Stimme geweckt: Die Schallplatte scheint uns ganz nah an die Ursprünge der musikalischen Kunst heranzuführen, in der Zwiesprache mit dem Komponisten allen Zufälligkeiten im Opernhaus entrückt.

Vielleicht ist darum der Anteil an Opernaufnahmen in einem Repertoire wie dem unseren so gross, entsprechend der Beliebtheit, die er bei Ihnen, verehrter Opernfreund, besitzt? Für Sie ist denn auch dieses Auswahlverzeichnis bestimmt, das auf den folgenden Seiten in alphabetischer Folge der Operntitel Gesamtaufnahmen, Querschnitte, Szenen und Arien aneinanderreiht, um Ihnen damit die Übersicht und das Suchen nach einzelnen Stücken zu erleichtern.

Ein Schallplatten-Repertoire ist der Spiegel eines jahrelangen Bemühens um künstlerische Qualität wie um weitestmögliche Vollständigkeit. Gerade unserem Hause haben dabei prominente Künstler von internationalem Rang zur Seite gestanden. So vielfältig Anlass und Entstehung einer Aufnahme auch gewesen sein mögen — sie hier angezeigt zu finden, bietet die Gewähr für einen ungetrübten musikalischen Genuss. Jede einzelne öffnet das Tor für den Zugang in das Zauberreich der Oper.

1

[65]

[66]

[67]

[68]

[65] A promotional leaflet for a live recording of *Arabella* (SLPM 138 883), at the Munich Opera in 1963.

[66]…[68] SLPM 138 690/91, recorded in Dresden's Lukaskirche in 1960. SLPM 138 390/91, recorded in 1957 at the Herkulessaal in Munich. SLPM 138 639/40, recorded in 1959 at the Herkulessaal in Munich.

[69]

[70]

[69]…[74] Karajan during rehearsals for the production of *Die Walküre* at the Salzburg Festival in 1967. The boxed set of the first part of the cycle (*Die Walküre*) was first recorded at the Jesus-Christus-Kirche in Berlin in 1966. Karajan generally gave staged productions at Salzburg after he had made the recorded version so as to spare the singers' voices, of which heavy demands were made on stage. He recorded the prologue (*Das Rheingold*) in 1967 in the same way, then the second and third parts (*Siegfried* and *Götterdämmerung* respectively) between 1968 and 1970.

[71]

[72]

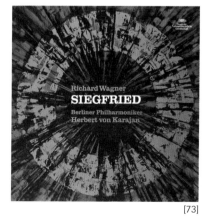

[73]

[74]

[75] Carlos Kleiber during the recording of *Tristan und Isolde* at the Lukaskirche in Dresden in 1980.

[76] LP 2741 009, recorded between 1980 and 1982 in Dresden, this legendary *Tristan*, conducted by Kleiber, features the sublime Welsh soprano Margaret Price in the role of Isolde, full of sweetness and femininity.

[77] LP 2740 152, recorded in 1976 at the Munich Opera.

[78] SLPM 138 931/33, recorded in 1964 at La Scala in Milan.

[79] CD 474 9742, recorded in 2003 at the Vienna State Opera. Conducting *Tristan und Isolde* has always been a privilege of the greatest maestros of this opera house. Following in the footsteps of Mahler, Furtwängler, Karajan, and Carlos Kleiber. Thielemann, in his turn, proved himself to be one of the greatest Wagnerian conductors of our time.

[75]

[76]

[77]

[78]

[79]

In 1967 Herbert von Karajan wished to present his orchestra with the indispensable experience of the orchestral pit. He created the Salzburg Easter Festival in order to achieve his life's ambition: a recording of Wagner's *Ring* under the best possible artistic conditions. Thanks to recording, what he considered at the time a state duty, and which corresponded to a thorough overhaul of the Wagnerian aesthetic, his wish found a sort of fulfillment. Never before had the master of Bayreuth's refinement of orchestration and transparency of different instrumental voices been expressed with such subtlety. The term *chamber music* was often applied to this by music critics of the period, who were too accustomed to noisier, more extrovert versions of the *Ring*. The Deutsche Grammophon aesthetic doubtless played a part in this, and the dynamic limitation that has already been discussed at length contributed to a somewhat pale sound compared with Decca/Solti's sound stage. The magnificent *Originals* remasterings, rereleased in 1998, finally provided the volume, transparency, and airiness that the LPs did not always succeed in reproducing; not to mention a dynamic and, to be frank, a power, and an impact, especially in *Götterdämmerung*, that challenge Decca's supposed supremacy.

In 1961 Deutsche Grammophon had signed a contract with La Scala of Milan for a series of recordings that became famous and would continue up until the end of the 1970s, with *Macbeth* and *Simon Boccanegra*, conducted by Abbado. Kubelik's renowned *Rigoletto* in 1964, with Dietrich Fischer-Dieskau in the title role, remains memorable. Carlos Kleiber entered the opera catalogue in 1973 with a *Freischütz*, which is still considered a model, followed by an extraordinary *Fledermaus*; musically masterful and technically supreme, these recordings remain some of Deutsche Grammophon's greatest successes. Klaus Scheibe knew how to produce recordings that are open, generous, airy, pleasing, and highly accurate with regard to timbre. Kleiber's mercurial conducting would also excel in *La Traviata* and finally in the beautiful, dreamlike digital recording of *Tristan* in 1981. Produced by Hans Hirsch with the talented Karl-August Naegler as recording engineer, the technology magically complements Kleiber's musical vision: the sonorities are warm, luminous, sometimes mellow (in the case of the Dresden strings), or thrustingly prominent when appropriate.

Other discs are also worthy of mention, such as the incomparable version of Richard Strauss's *Die Frau ohne Schatten*, conducted by Joseph Keilberth in Munich, and *Arabella*, recorded in 1963. In 1969, in Dresden, Karl Böhm recorded a fine *Fidelio* that is energetic, spontaneous, and refined. These are all exceptional musical accounts. In the 1980s, special mention goes to Bernstein's wonderful *West Side Story*, enhanced by recording that is in a class of its own, with its absolute clarity and lack of any harshness; his delightful *Candide* is in the same vein. More recently, Messiaen's *Saint François d'Assise*, recorded at Salzburg in 1999, deserves to be mentioned; the excitement of a live performance exerts its full appeal, as does Abbado's studio recording of *Falstaff* of 2001, which allows us to hear the Berlin Philharmonic in its full power and magnificence as an opera orchestra. Christian Thielemann deliberately attempted, with considerable success, to associate *Tristan* with elements of the past in 2003, and again in 2005 with *Parsifal*: the live recordings from the Staatsoper in Vienna features superb sound that is warm, engaging, and sumptuously recorded, as does the recent Salzburg *Traviata* of 2006.

LEONARD BERNSTEIN: THE UNION OF NEW YORK AND VIENNA

Although Karl Böhm was, in truth, Herbert von Karajan's real rival, sharing the same musical culture and a relatively similar and circumscribed repertoire, Karajan's media rival was Leonard Bernstein. The American conductor made his first recording for Deutsche Grammophon in 1972 with Bizet's *Carmen*. Setting out to conquer musical Europe, Bernstein wanted above all to reteach Mahler, neglected in Vienna for many decades, to the Vienna Philharmonic, and he did so with some success. Most of his official recordings released by Deutsche Grammophon would be drawn from the maestro's live recordings, which, consequently, are notable for their thrilling spontaneity.

Compared with the Beethoven, Brahms, and Schumann cycles, which are rather conventional, the Mahler, recorded with several orchestras (the Vienna Philharmonic, the Amsterdam Concertgebouw, and the New York Philharmonic), is one of the most convincing in the whole discography. Symphony no. 5 (Vienna), recorded in 1985 at Frankfurt's Alte Oper, dominates the cycle with the sheer beauty of sound and music, thanks in part to the engineering of Karl-August Naegler, who would be responsible for Bernstein's most beautiful recordings. Silky strings, mellow woodwind, and an incredible vitality and impressive dynamic range reveal the unique sound of the Vienna Philharmonic in top form.

There is also an exceptional, somewhat earlier tribute to the maestro's wife, Felicia Montealegre, who had recently died: the version for string orchestra of Beethoven's Quartet op. 131, a work that Bernstein prized above all others. Recorded very close to the players, this vertiginous, blazing live recording—quite irresistible—stands out for its almost tangible presence. This large chamber orchestra is staggering in its fervor and involvement and shows Bernstein and Vienna at their best, as do their magnificent Shostakovich recordings (in particular Symphony no. 6), recorded late in his career.

Special mention should be made of two of Bernstein's final recordings: the Sibelius Symphony no. 1 of 1990, probably the most beautiful account of the work by Bernstein, a conductor with a nearly unequalled ability to unleash the Vienna orchestra's full intensity. This live recording demonstrates astonishing sound quality, thanks once again to the talent of Karl-August Naegler. Finally the overwhelming, almost obsessed, Bruckner Symphony no. 9 seems to belong to another world.

DEUTSCHE GRAMMOPHON AND THE PIANO

Wilhelm Kempff, Deutsche Grammophon's great postwar pianist, completed his first cycle of the Beethoven sonatas in 1950, followed by the concertos, conducted by Paul van Kempen. The arrival of stereo prompted him to make some improvements to the same concertos in the 1960s, this time conducted by Ferdinand Leitner. This was followed by a new recording of the sonatas, of course, and then by a Schubert cycle, released in 1969, along with works by Schumann.

[80]

[81]

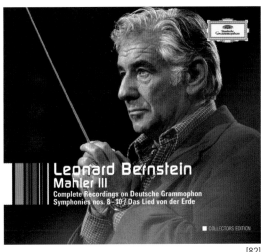

[82]

[83]

[84]

[80]…[84] The 2005 rerelease, in the *Collectors Edition*, of the complete symphonies of Mahler. Toward the end of his life, Leonard Bernstein had a preference for live recordings, as they are more spontaneous than those made in a studio.

[85] [86] Vladimir Horowitz returned to his native Russia after sixty-one years of absence to give recitals in Moscow and Leningrad—the recital in Moscow in 1986 was transmitted live on television in Western Europe and the United States, and prerecorded for the rest of the world.

[87] The little-known sleeve of Martha Argerich's first record: SLPM 138 672, recorded in the Beethovensaal in Hanover in 1960.

[88] LP 2530 155, recorded in 1971.

[89] LP 2530 291, recorded in 1972.

[90] Arturo Benedetti Michelangeli, a private and solitary pianist whose recordings with Deutsche Grammophon were epochal.

[91] Russian pianist Emil Gilels (1916–1985) was one of the greatest performers of Beethoven and Brahms.

[85]

[86]

[87]

[88]

[89]

[90]

[91]

It is unsettling to note the degree to which a certain Deutsche Grammophon aesthetic perfectly espoused Kempff's highly characteristic sound, which frustrated certain listeners: the very marked restraint of the bass and an articulated upper register of infinite delicacy, yet still percussive, was at the opposite extreme of the Decca sound of the same period, which was opulent with great harmonic richness in the lower end of the spectrum, and sometimes even slightly harsh, if we think of Julius Katchen's Brahms recordings. But curiously, Deutsche Grammophon's sound, somewhat limited in bandwidth as in dynamics, suits this almost translucent aesthetic rather well; it always has great integrity and is imbued with a near-feminine poetry.

The pianists represented by the Yellow Label are legion, from Richter early on, to Lang Lang today, by way of Martha Argerich from 1960, Géza Anda, Maurizio Pollini, Emil Gilels, a few records by Dino Ciani (the first of which was released in the short-lived *Début* collection), Ivo Pogorelich, Rudolf Serkin, Arturo Benedetti Michelangeli, Vladimir Horowitz and, more recently, Anatol Ugorsky, Evgeny Kissin, Mikhail Pletnev, Hélène Grimaud, and numerous others. The uniqueness of the Deutsche Grammophon sound is well suited to the touch of certain pianists. So, after Maurizio Pollini's renewed success, Deutsche Grammophon decided to record his first disc, the Chopin *Études*, in 1972. The sound is as limpid as water, but the very percussive piano of the Italian musician is surprising: the recording highlights the clearness of attack, lacking superfluous bass and, in the final analysis, opulence. The quest for the right timbre, dear to this Italian pianist, who is known to be very attached to the music of his time, has continued for over three decades up to the present day. Boasting unprecedented, almost alchemic subtlety, Arturo Benedetti Michelangeli's playing called for microphones capable of capturing the slightest musical inflection and sensitive to the slightest change of color. From this point of view, Debussy's *Images* remain a model performance, enhanced by the great accuracy of the recording.

Finally, it is impossible not to mention the king of pianists, Vladimir Horowitz. His mastery was perhaps incomparable, but at the same time the American musician's playing was uniquely personal, rather like Karajan's conducting in the sphere of the orchestra. His superior technique allowed him to envisage works beyond a given or imposed stylistic constraint. In his famous *Moscow Concert*, recorded live in 1985, the master's incredible touch, sometimes immeasurably delicate and calculated, sometimes quite tongue-in-cheek, is fascinating. The microphones, placed quite close to the instrument, emphasize the extreme sophistication of his playing.

FROM ANALOG TO DIGITAL

In the late 1970s, during a Japanese tour, Herbert von Karajan was invited by Akio Morita, the president of Sony, to a private hearing of the digital recording of *Il Trovatore* that he had just conducted at the Vienna Staatsoper. Captivated by the beauty of the sound and the dynamic range and spatial imaging, the maestro demanded that, from then on, all his discs make use of this new technique. This would be put into practice the use of a famous original system, developed by the American firm 3M, that took into account that digital recordings would first be released on LP and not on CD.

In 1980 Deutsche Grammophon released *The Magic Flute* conducted by Karajan, which was in fact somewhat disappointing from a strictly audio

[92]

[93]

[94]

[95]

[96]

[92] … [97] Whether recordings of his own compositions or other twentieth-century classics, those made by Pierre Boulez constitute one of the most beautiful discographies of contemporary music released by Deutsche Grammophon. Today, he remains one of the company's major artists.

[97]

point of view: the sounds were somewhat harsh, not vibrant, and the spatial impression was somewhat constricted. In short, the result was less convincing than that obtained in the finest analog recordings made in the late 1970s by Böhm in Vienna, Ozawa in Boston, or Giulini in Chicago. Things soon improved with a sublime *Parsifal*, which was a great success in every respect. But the LP, analog by nature, did not manage to fully reproduce the supposed splendor of digital sound. The CD made its presence felt quite quickly—in 1982 to be precise—with Richard Strauss's *Alpine Symphony*, again under Karajan. The absence of hiss and the overall cleanness of sound were striking. On the other hand, some expert ears deplored a certain sterility, if not glare, that could prove trying during long hours of listening.

A debate arose, which has not since died down, between the supporters of the LP, who are in favor of a more natural, more sensual—in a word, more musical—reproduction, and those who prefer more perfect listening conditions, devoid of the mechanical friction imposed by the contact and consequent wear of the groove from the movement of the stylus. A number of CDs released in the 1980s lacked definition and consequently thinness, and this lack often resulted in sound that could sometimes be harsh, metallic, and somewhat unpleasant. At Deutsche Grammophon, the advent of the "4-D Audio-Recording" process was decisive in terms of added sound value, producing heightened dynamics, a remarkably homogeneous bandwidth, and tremendous transparency. This was a totally digital recording method, from the preamplifier of the remote-controlled microphones to the mixing, which used 21-bit analog-digital conversion for optimal resolution, and finally to the "stage box," which enabled the sound signal to be transmitted without analogue interruption. At that time, Deutsche Grammophon clearly won out over direct competitors in terms of recording technique. The Boulez recordings perfectly illustrate the excellence that had been achieved at the beginning of the 1990s and that would remain unchallenged until very recent, further advances in technology at the Emile Berliner Studios in Hanover.

PIERRE BOULEZ: FROM VIENNA TO CLEVELAND VIA BERLIN AND CHICAGO

The death of Karajan in July 1989 left a considerable gap and imposed new rules. Pierre Boulez, who had long been recording for the Yellow Label, beginning with *Parsifal* in 1970, was called upon to rerecord his favorite repertoire: the wellsprings of twentieth-century music and the major works stemming from it, including works by Debussy, Ravel, Varèse, and Messiaen for French music, along with Bartók, Stravinsky, Schoenberg, Webern, and Mahler. The world's leading orchestras shared the task to ensure a perfect match between the selected works and the style, color, and musical culture of each of the ensembles: the Cleveland Orchestra's flexibility and near-French precision for Debussy and Ravel; the Chicago Symphony Orchestra's power and perfection for Bartók; the Berlin Philharmonic's sensuality for Ravel and Webern; and the Vienna Philharmonic's incomparable musicality for what would be the finest segments of the Mahler cycle. In most cases, the sound quality, meticulously controlled by the conductor and by Rainer Maillard and Karl-August Naegler, is striking. The quality and purity of Cleveland's timbres in Debussy's *Images* are impressive, revealing a transparency of sound until then unknown, and are matched by Chicago's quality and stability in Bartók's *Wooden Prince* and the equally incomparable Varèse disc.

And then there is the Mahler cycle, without a doubt dominated by the Symphony no. 6, recorded in Vienna, as were nos. 2, 3, and 5 and *Das Lied von der Erde*. Rainer Maillard skillfully succeeded in extracting a sound that belongs uniquely to Mahler and Vienna—and that some had believed lost since the death of Bruno Walter—with luminous strings, a harmonic richness in the upper register, and singularly resonant basses.

DEUTSCHE GRAMMOPHON AND CONTEMPORARY MUSIC

In the 1950s the two famous *Musica Nova* sets of six mono discs highlighted the great European—but especially German—composers of the period: Stockhausen, Henze, Blacher, Fortner, Hartmann, and Egk, along with Stravinsky, Bartók, and numerous others. After a ten-year hiatus, Deutsche Grammophon returned to this theme, launching the famous *avant garde* collection, a series of four sets released between the autumn of 1968 and the autumn of 1971. These twenty-four discs covered a wide range of the contemporary music of the time, featuring milestone works, such as Stockhausen's *Stimmung* and pieces by Ligeti, Nono, Bussotti, Kagel, Cage, Zimmermann, and Holliger. These sets, distributed to a somewhat limited audience, were distinguished by first-class manufacturing and sound quality. At the same time, Deutsche Grammophon undertook the recording of Stockhausen's complete works in near-ideal technical conditions. To be convinced of this, it is enough to listen to the famous *Momente* or to the opera *Donnerstag aus "Licht."*

Other albums, also of considerable interest, followed, including Bussotti's *Rara Requiem*, one of Deutsche Grammophon's finest analog recordings, to the credit of Heinz Wildhagen. Certain recordings, such as Berio's *Coro*, would reappear in the excellent *20/21* collection issued in the past few years, noteworthy on more than one account and a magnificent echo of the *avant garde* collection. Even though *20/21* contains many reissues, new releases are hardly lacking, and the series is dominated by the fabulous *Sequenze* by Berio and the Ensemble Intercontemporain, Boulez's *Le Marteau sans maître* and *Répons*, by the composer, and Messiaen's *Saint François*.

DISCOVERY AND REDISCOVERY WITH THE ORIGINALS SERIES

In 1995 Deutsche Grammophon released the first recordings in the *Originals* series. These were analog recordings from the 1950s, 1960s, and 1970s, restored using "Original-Image-Bit-Processing" technology. This ambitious digital restoration was intended to re-create, with unprecedented fidelity, the original sound image of these often-legendary interpretations from Deutsche Grammophon's Golden Age. The convincing results, as previously mentioned, often surpass the ostensible potential of the original LPs.

Although a number of these reissues have a slight acidity—an endemic characteristic of the label—there are also some extremely fine recordings that are clearly superior to the LPs or the first CD editions. To cite some examples: the ineffably beautiful Brahms piano concertos by Gilels and Jochum with a transcendent Berlin Philharmonic; numerous Karajan recordings, including the Honegger disc, Prokofiev's Symphony no. 5 and the Brahms Symphony no. 1 of 1964; certain Beethoven recordings by Böhm, including the *Pastoral* Symphony, Symphony no. 7, and the *Coriolan* Overture; Mahler's Symphony no. 1 by Kubelik; Prokofiev's

[98]

[99]

[100]

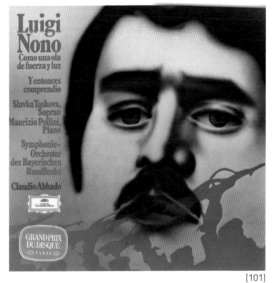

[101]

[102]

[103]

[98] [99] The two Stockhausen recordings *Momente* and *Sirius* which appeared in 1975 and 1980 respectively, are collector's items. Today, Deutsche Grammophon has never managed to rerelease these two 33 rpm records on CD.

[100]...[102] Volume 3 of the *avant garde* boxed set appeared in 1970, another rarity of contemporary repertoire that is much sought after by discophiles, as are these Nono (1974) and Bussoti (1976) records.

[103] The *20/21* series, devoted to contemporary music, as was the *avant garde* series, is also visually distinctive: the original and very modern design of its covers distinguishes them from the sleeves of classical repertoire albums.

[104]

[105]

[106]

[107]

[104] … [109] The Emile Berliner studios, based in Hanover, carefully preserve Deutsche Grammophon's original analog sound recordings. It is from these that it creates, using state-of-the-art technology, the famous remasterings of the *Originals* series. Archiv Producktion and Deutsche Grammophon contemporary artists, such as the star duo Villazón and Netrebko (here in *La Traviata*) and the promising and talented Measha Brueggergosman, also benefit from this technology.

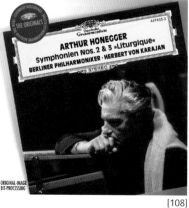

[108]

[109]

Alexander Nevsky by Abbado; and the incredible last three Tchaikovsky symphonies by Mravinsky, which reveal a staggering, previously unknown spatial definition, though it is true that the latter, rereleased in 2006, further benefited from the services of the new Emile Berliner Studios.

FROM 4-D TO THE EMILE BERLINER STUDIOS

The Emile Berliner Studios, now a company independent from Deutsche Grammophon, complete the final stage in digital reproduction. The studio's cutting-edge technology can produce the finest quality possible in terms of remastering from old analog archives. For several years now, Deutsche Grammophon has relied on the Emile Berliner Studios to obtain literally unheard-of results in terms of sound realism.

Noteworthy among many outstanding recordings are the magnificent *Traviata* with an incredibly close Netrebko/Villazón duet. Among the great orchestral recordings, the prodigious dynamics and bandwidth of Richard Strauss's *Heldenleben* by Thielemann, recorded in Vienna, are truly impressive, and Mahler's Symphonie no. 3 by Boulez, also recorded in Vienna, released in stereo but also in multichannel, a recording technique that seems to have been abandoned. Measha Brueggergosman's recent delightful *Surprise*, an album of cabaret music, conforms to this rule of unrestricted dynamics and limpidity, totally devoid of any sonic veil. Finally, the *Master Recordings* series, released in 2008 to celebrate the centenary of Karajan's birth, give particular luster to recordings made in the 1960s: Karajan's recordings of Beethoven's Symphony no. 4 of 1962 and Stravinsky's *Rite of Spring* of 1964 have never had such intensity and clarity, combined with a lack of harshness; a result previously believed impossible to achieve.

In his essay *The Work of Art in the Age of Mechanical Reproduction*, Walter Benjamin discusses, at length, the technical reproducibility of the visual or sonic work of art, and the famous loss of "aura," a phenomenon, in his opinion, unavoidable with reproduction techniques. A recording will never replace a concert, yet it must be admitted that recordings, such as the *Ring* by Karajan; Haydn's *Creation*, for which Dietrich Fischer-Dieskau, Gundula Janowitz, and Fritz Wunderlich worked together; Bruckner's Symphony no. 7 or Beethoven's *Pastoral* Symphony by Böhm; Debussy's *Images* by Michelangeli; the Horowitz in Moscow concert, Mahler's Symphony no. 9 by Giulini, or Sibelius's Symphony no. 1 by Bernstein now belong to a "museum without walls" of a new, somehow magical kind, which live music is unable to supplant.

HEINZ WILDHAGEN
Recording Engineer and Producer

You joined Deutsche Grammophon in 1951 and left in 1983 but continued recording for the Yellow Label until 1987. How did you want the recording of Mahler's symphonies conducted by Rafael Kubelik to be heard?
I wanted to hear the music exactly as it is set out on the score. Without a precise understanding of the score, you cannot produce a recording that is true to the composer's conception. It's totally unsatisfactory to begin a recording without thorough preparation. This was all the more true for Gustav Mahler's symphonies, which, at the time of the Kubelik recording, had rarely been played in concert.

How many microphones did you use, and where did you place them?
The number of microphones used depends on the acoustic quality of the venue in which you are recording and also on the type of music being recorded. As all of the Mahler symphonies (except for no. 8) were recorded in the Herkulessaal, additional microphones were only required to record particular instruments, the soloists, and the choir. Symphony no. 8 was recorded in the Deutsche Museum's concert hall as the Herkulessaal was too small to house all those involved. I should add that I always aimed to work with the least number of microphones possible.

How would you describe the sound produced by Karajan and Hermanns?
I don't actually have much to say about how Karajan and Hermanns worked together as I was never there. The fact that Karajan wanted to play a whole variety of works during some sessions must certainly have made things difficult. It would have been well-nigh impossible to come up with the appropriate recording technology to handle such varied content. This is my only explanation for several of the results, which, as far as sound is concerned, are not exactly convincing. However, as far as I am aware, Karajan never complained about this.

Can we say that there is a specific Deutsche Grammophon sound?
We can't say that there was a specific Deutsche Grammophon sound. In fact, I have always tried to portray the specific acoustic features of each particular orchestra. If the orchestra was recorded in its usual concert hall, I would try to bring out the orchestra's particular features on the recording. I couldn't understand why it was sometimes expected that all orchestras should sound the same. If this was the case, why work with different ensembles at all? Just as a soloist can be distinguished by his voice, it should be possible to recognize individual orchestras. The limitations of the 40dB dynamic range that existed at the time should also be taken into account. The laws of physics state that music is played less dynamically in rooms with considerable echo, so recordings were often made in churches, as this meant that you barely had to compress the dynamics at all on the mixing desk. The quality of a recording depends, of course, at any time on the quality of the equipment used and the skills of the recording staff.

RAINER HÖPFNER
Recording Engineer, member of Steering Committee of Emile Berliner Studios

You joined Deutsche Grammophon in 1977 and were responsible for the technical part of the recordings. From 1978 you were involved with nearly all of Herbert von Karajan's recordings. What are the functions of the recorder you used?
The recorder was the 3M DMS M81 and was a 32-track digital audio recorder. We used this system for location recordings and editing in the studio. Previously, we had worked with analog 8- and 16-track recorders. With this 3M recorder system, we could take advantage of digital recording technology.

Why was this device so important for Deutsche Grammophon technology, and how did it come to be used in its recording production process?
The first recordings with this machine took place in 1978/79. It was the first digital 32-channel multitrack recorder system that allowed us to edit, which was essential for the Deutsche Grammophon–recording workflow. At Deutsche Grammophon, the multitrack tapes were edited, and later on, the final mix was done from this master tape. Our four recorders were used for all multitrack recordings from this time on. There was a special Deutsche Grammophon–designed system using these digital recorders for the Telemondial video projects.

Why was it so important for Herbert von Karajan?
Herbert von Karajan liked to work with the latest technology and highest quality available, so at that time, we needed to use this recording system.

Can you recall some examples of recordings made with this machine?
From 1978 nearly all recordings with Herbert von Karajan were made with these multitrack recorders. The final mix was recorded later in the studios on the Sony 2-track U-matic system.

How long did the 3M recorder remain a technological asset?
We changed the recording system for the recording of the New Year's Day concert in Vienna in 1987. For this event, we used the multitrack recorder Sony 3324. This recorder replaced the 3M recorders at Deutsche Grammophon because it offered nearly the same features we needed for our projects, and at this time 3M couldn't deliver support anymore and didn't have an updated system available. The Sony machine used the latest, state-of-the-art technology—for example, improved analog-to-digital and digital-to-analog converters. The newer Sony recorders were much easier to handle, and the sound quality was better, thanks to the new converter generation. The multitrack tapes from the 3M recorders were digitally transferred onto the Sony system using a Deutsche Grammophon–designed decoder.

RAINER MAILLARD

Producer and Recording Engineer, Professor at the Detmold Conservatory for Music

You joined the Deutsche Grammophon Recording Center, later renamed Emile Berliner Studios. Over the past twenty years, you have made outstanding recordings, such as Pierre Boulez's Bartók and the wonderful Ravel concertos with Krystian Zimerman. What is your secret?

I don't have any secrets. I have just been lucky to be able to work in extremely good conditions. It's like a good meal: first you need good ingredients, then the right utensils and knowledge of how to prepare the ingredients. The rest is a question of craftsmanship, experience, taste, and the capacity to precisely fulfill customers' expectations. As a recording engineer, I am never exclusively responsible for sound. Let's take the example you mentioned of Ravel's piano concerto with Krystian Zimerman. The music was performed by first-class musicians. Before the recording was made, the work had been played several times in various concerts. The Steinway had been tuned especially for the work, and the acoustics in the recording venue were perfect. The technology operated flawlessly; there was ample time both for production and postproduction. When we put all of these individual elements together, it's really not so hard to produce wonderful results. It's a lot harder to produce the same results when working under less perfect conditions, in which case I have to dig a lot deeper into my bag of tricks.

How do you explain the difference in dynamics between the LP and the CD?

All technology has its advantages but also its limitations. Whether producing an analog vinyl record or a digital compact disc, as a recording engineer I am always able to make the medium sound more or less dynamic. A good recording is never determined by one single parameter. There is always a chain of several factors that influence the sound. Part of the recording engineer's role is to ensure that the listener cannot detect any limitations. CD production involves more advanced sound technology. Microphones, mixing desks, and recording quality are constantly evolving. This makes it harder to pinpoint one single parameter as being responsible for improving sound quality.

The remastering of *the Originals* is remarkable. With this new discovery, the standard of sound in these recordings is truly outstanding, for example in Karajan's *Ring* or his interpretation of Prokofiev's Symphony no. 5.

Our aim in remastering these recordings was to produce the best-ever sound quality. There were no tricks involved; it was just a matter of following a number of simple and clear steps. Analog and digital technical enhancements really helped us. For example, in the late 1970s, all Deutsche Grammophon productions were recorded using one tape recorder with four sound tracks. That was the norm for the quadraphonic process used at the time. To cut a conventional LP, stereo balance had to be created first, i.e., a further tape recording was made, and four tracks were mixed down to two. Unfortunately, this also created greater distortion and more noise. For the remastered version, we skipped this step because it was easier to copy it in the digital domain without quality loss. To sum up, many small improvements, by themselves barely audible, are brought together to produce a wonderful overall result.

In the 1990s, you took part in the *Karajan Gold* collection. What is your feeling about this tremendous CD series?

The late Karajan recordings were all made in the early years of digital audio. Record-company marketing departments were often far quicker to advertise new technological advances before recording engineers had converted to their use. Huge developments were made in sound technology at this time, and shortly after Karajan's death, more technology became available, making audible improvements possible. We subsequently used these new techniques for the *Karajan Gold* collection and were even able to enhance the original recording by editing out occasional instrumental "splits" which had gone undetected.

Four years ago, you recorded a beautiful *Traviata* in Salzburg. It was a multitrack recording. Do you think this standard brings something more than stereo?

A successful recording is only ever an illusion created using technology. It draws the listener into the music, carries him along, and seduces him. How well that works does not necessarily depend on the number of loudspeakers. Even in the kitchen or the car, we can be stirred by music played through simple, one-dimensional speakers. However, the listener can experience more pleasure by listening to music on top-quality equipment. And spatial playback also improves our understanding of the musical structure. Fifty years ago, the first step was made from mono to stereo. With mono playback, sound comes out of a single loudspeaker—all of the musical information is superimposed onto a single point. The acoustic pattern becomes more expanded with stereophonic playback, when two loudspeakers are used. It's easier to differentiate between individual instruments as the sound reaches the listener sitting in his living room from different directions. A soft melody is easier to hear if it is not concealed by louder instruments coming from the same direction. If five, instead of two, playback channels, are used, this effect can be increased further.

For example, a few years ago we produced Gustav Mahler's Symphony no. 3 with the Vienna Philharmonic, conducted by Pierre Boulez in the Vienna Musikverein. For the usual stereo sound mix, I would set up the main microphones in front of the orchestra and place an array of spot microphones amidst the instruments. By skillfully mixing the individual support microphones in relation to the main microphone, I achieve the required sound balance for a stereo mix. While recording the Mahler symphony, I discovered that, with a few exceptions, I could actually do the surround mix without the support microphones. The main microphone system was perfectly adequate. The sound was far more transparent and clear when played back over five loudspeakers and meant that spot microphones were not necessary. But even surround sound played over five loudspeakers is not true to the live sound experience. In a concert hall, sound reaches us from all directions, whereas when played back through loudspeakers, the three-dimensional element always appears to be reduced. Nevertheless, or perhaps rather thanks to this, many wonderful illusions can be achieved.

The *Traviata* production that you mention was planned as a CD and DVD version right from the start. 5.1 surround sound has established itself as the norm for DVDs. And it is likely that there will be sound-recording media with even more channels in the future. For this reason, we have been recording all productions on multitrack recorders for years so that we can offer different mixes depending on the loudspeaker system used.

[]

GÜNTHER BREEST

Former Executive Vice President, Former Artist and Repertoire Director,
Deutsche Grammophon

You joined Deutsche Grammophon in 1970 as a producer and left the company in 1988 as executive vice president and A&R department director. What was your artistic policy?
More precisely, I joined Deutsche Grammophon in October 1970 as a producer with assigned artists, such as Eugen Jochum and the Amadeus Quartet. My responsibility at the time was the planning and actual recording of projects as recording supervisor, and I sometimes worked as a recording engineer at the same time. At Deutsche Grammophon's sister label Philips Classics, these two functions were always combined, and the producer was responsible for managerial duties only. Deutsche Grammophon had traditionally split responsibilities between the balance engineer at the desk and the artistic supervisor as a partner of the performer. All postproduction work had to be done at the studios in Hanover. More and more, I felt that I was most efficiently employed in planning and negotiating deals—as a result, I was promoted over time into a management function as head of A&R.

In the 1970s the Deutsche Grammophon label was still very much identified as a "German" label, with a strong reputation for quality. The yellow cartouche stood for the best recording quality, sophisticated packaging, and the finest artists. The time seemed right to develop Deutsche Grammophon into a number-one label internationally. Without losing what had been achieved so far, we had to build a more international artist roster.

I realized that there were certain reservations in the international Jewish artistic community about working with a record company that even had the name "Deutsche" Grammophon on its labels. We had to win back trust, and I felt, as a young ambitious German producer, that this was my duty. I was successful, in the end, signing great artists, such as Milstein, Barenboim, the Israel Philharmonic, Zukerman, and Perlman, to name just a few. The first signing with Perlman took place at the pool at the Tel Aviv Hilton.

Another major task was the development of opera recordings to compete with other labels. Abbado's Verdi recordings with the forces of La Scala and Karajan's *Tosca* were breakthroughs, and important signings such as Domingo, Ricciarelli, Carreras, Raimondi, and others followed. Within ten years, Deutsche Grammophon was considered to be the leading classical label in the world, with both Bernstein and Karajan under contract at the same time—not always an easy task because both had tremendous personalities. But Karajan was restricted in recording only with the Berlin Philharmonic and the Vienna Philharmonic and also started his own film project, culminating in the creation of *His Legacy for Home Video*. Bernstein focused on rerecording his own works (including *West Side Story*) and was presented as an international conductor in front of the Israel Philharmonic as well as the Concertgebouw, the Vienna Philharmonic, and the London Symphony Orchestra; most of these projects were live telecasts in connection with Unitel. So the profiles of the two artists were compatible but had to be managed very carefully.

196

Can you describe the evolution of the Deutsche Grammophon sound?
The sound quality of the Yellow Label has always been considered traditional. The most powerful artist was, of course, Herbert von Karajan, and his aesthetics—beautiful blending, no sharpness or aggressiveness—had a huge influence. Decca, had always been more adventurous, for example in their stage-sound opera recordings. For years after the merger of Decca and PolyGram, the technical departments were strictly separated and it was impossible for a Deutsche Grammophon team to use Decca's equipment, even when there was a recording planned in London. The solidity and reliability of Deutsche Grammophon products were, nevertheless, a trademark, and the yellow cartouche made them easy to identify in the marketplace.

What in your opinion are the main differences between Deutsche Grammophon and the other labels?
Quality in manufacturing and presentation have been the distinguishing marks of Deutsche Grammophon from the beginning. Very sophisticated in-house teams in marketing, editorial, design and artwork, artist promotion and press relations, A&R, legal and business affairs, secondary rights and, last but not least, the great recording teams in Hanover, were actually the reasons for our success. All this culminated at the beginning of the 1980s with the invention of the CD, which resulted in a new generation of recordings with the finest artists around. That made Deutsche Grammophon even stronger than before.

What was your policy for the preparation of a new generation of artists?
In my years as head of A&R, the development of new, young talent was a central focus. Around the world in all major markets, local marketing organizations were very active and demanding. Frequent International meetings were a great opportunity to overview the development of outstanding young talents. Major competitions were good sources for careful selection and integration into the existing artist roster—Krystian Zimerman, Ivo Pogorelich, and Shlomo Mintz, to name a few, were signed in this way. And the artist promotion department did an extremely good job. But to be fair, there was still a great distribution system existing, with quite a number of specialized classical-record shops, where artist information and promotional material could be displayed.

What do you think about the evolution of the classical music industry?
I have a wonderful memory of a concert that I experienced with Sviatoslav Richter years ago—a small concert hall with dimmed light, a small lamp next to the piano, and Schubert played divinely. Have those times gone forever? A great loss, of course, but to be honest, I am not sure that if concerts were to be performed today with this kind of intimacy, the music industry would be able to survive.

[01]

[02]

[03]

[04]

[05]

[06]

[07]

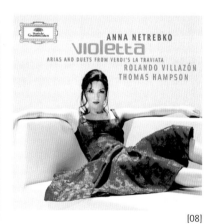

[08]

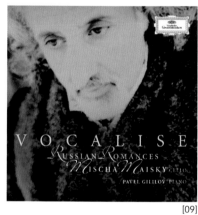

[09]

[10]

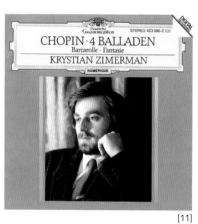

[11]

[12]

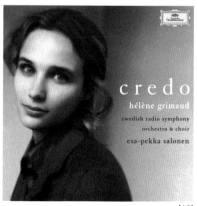

[13]

DEUTSCHE GRAMMOPHON'S VISUAL COMMUNICATION: BETWEEN APOLLO AND DIONYSUS

OLIVIER BORUCHOWITCH

The Deutsche Grammophon label sets the standard for the classical-record industry. Its commercial development, focused on Europe from the end of the 1950s, has become global since the 1970s, thanks to the strength of PolyGram's distribution network, and this has coincided with a particularly favorable era for the mass distribution of classical music.

Granted, at the beginning of the thirty-year postwar boom, the circle of classical music consumers consisted primarily of initiates and was the near-exclusive preserve of enlightened and well-off music lovers. But the progressive emergence of the middle class and, above all, the extraordinary development in technological-distribution methods, enabled the classical repertoire to break out of the confines of the concert hall and opera house and reach a much wider audience. Thanks to radio, television, and the mass availability of record-playing equipment, great music was within everyone's grasp. From the car radio to the stereo system, from the television to the theater and, some forty years later, from the CD to the DVD to the iPod and digital downloading, the contacts between music and its audience have multiplied and become more diverse.

The commercialization of works from the classical repertoire observes the same rules governing all consumer products, and image policy has played a fundamental role in Deutsche Grammophon's identity. How has the label positioned itself within its market segment? How has it managed the image of its artists? The issue is all the more interesting in that the various options that the label has chosen reflect important developments in the classical-record industry and refer to the mixed reception that society overall has given it in these past decades. We can distinguish two major periods, coinciding with two revolutions in the democratization of access to culture. In the first, in its visual communication, Deutsche Grammophon maintained the exclusive, aristocratic features inherited from tradition. In the second, in contrast, it has sought to erase them.

APOLLONIAN NEOCLASSICISM

The care lavished on the concept and illustration of covers has always been an essential feature of Deutsche Grammophon policy; its instantly identifiable trademark is now part of the collective cultural heritage. The symbolic significance of the CD cover or record jacket was championed by Pali Meller Marcovicz, the great orchestrator of this policy. This was to be an extension of the technological excellence and artistic quality that have ensured the label's international reputation. The aesthetic principles and choices that had thus governed the integration and coherence of a personal style were applied to a two-part strategy: the short-term commercial objective, based on the product's strong visual identity, was coupled with a long-term institutional perspective, aimed at linking the interpretation of the work to Deutsche Grammophon, as represented by its famous cartouche.

This subtle association, created by juxtaposing the illustration with the famous record company's visual identity, was embodied in the omnipresence of the cartouche above the photo of the artist, painting, or objet d'art relating to the program on the disc, like the poster for a show or concert. For full-price discs, the cartouche could occupy up to a quarter of the upper space of the cover, with the name of the composer and the work generally given greater emphasis than that of the artists or ensembles, indicating that the artistic policy was directed toward the repertoire. In most cases, the presence of the performer was underscored by the image on the cover.

The seriousness of the photographs preferred by Deutsche Grammophon up until the 1990s was far from insignificant: it indicated the choices and positioning strategy pursued by the company until then, based on a dominant model. It was an era when the paradigmatic figure of visual communication was the conductor, who had traditionally been the driving force in the development of Deutsche Grammophon's artistic profile. It was, therefore, a matter of using an image that emphasized the distance between the artist and the public—a respectful, carefully calculated distance, illustrated by either a portrait in a real-life situation or a staged photo of the conductor practising his art.

The neoclassicism pursued by Pali Meller Marcovicz and his team emphasized the values of seriousness, moderation, proportion, and rigor. It is no coincidence that this aesthetic particularly echoed what Hebert von Karajan strove for in his conducting. The covers were a perfect illustration of this distancing, conveying the artist's gravity and mystique. This image governed how other great conductors, such as Karl Böhm, Leonard Bernstein, Carlos Kleiber, Carlo Maria Giulini, and Giuseppe Sinopoli, as well as major performers, such as Martha Argerich, Géza Anda, Dietrich Fischer-Dieskau, or Cheryl Studer would be portrayed. The iconography also matched the profile of the Deutsche Grammophon target audience: city-dwelling, middle-aged, rather bourgeois, cultivated, and conservative. They expected a certain reserve from the artist in keeping with the function assigned to him, i.e., as interpreter of the traditional heritage. This visual matrix focusing on the conductor expressed this distance, heightening the isolation of the artist, who faces away from the listener. Let us not forget that the conductor is the only performer who keeps his back turned to the audience; he is a constant reminder that the spectator remains an individual who cannot connect with the work by himself, because the conductor is the necessary intermediary through whom it is passed on. The Apollonian centrality in the aesthetic of the image and the cover marked Deutsche Grammophon's policy over a long period of time, effectively illustrating the positioning of the label and the values that it had long proclaimed.

THE DIONYSIAN REVOLUTION

This paradigm, which generally dominated until the 1990s, has progressively lost its validity, both for reasons external to Deutsche Grammophon, attributable to changes in the perception of classical music by society, and for internal reasons. In 1990 the Three Tenors concert with Luciano Pavarotti, Plácido Domingo, and José Carreras, broadcast from Rome by numerous television networks, was a worldwide success and led to a phenomenal increase in similar events. The immediate success of this new genre multiplied, and the organization of concerts, recitals, and operas in ever-vaster venues quickly became commonplace.

The shift from the figure of the conductor to that of the singer or instrumentalist considerably influenced the constants that had governed the world of classical music until then. This world had to assimilate several important, previously unheard-of notions, and some ideas that had remained as elite survivors from its more distant past would be forced to disappear.

Excess had made a conspicuous entrance: disproportion became the norm in the size of the concert venue as well as in television broadcasts, which became almost worldwide. Another fundamental shift was the fact that the opera singer, unlike the conductor, always faces the hall and is in permanent contact with the audience. The policy of distance was, therefore, no longer viable; on the contrary, the notion of a relationship became essential and, moreover, offered all the possible variants of passion, emotion, and feeling that interpretation requires. In other words, with the emergence of a communication centered on the performer, proximity became fundamental and replaced distance. It was no longer individualism but, on the contrary, identification, fusion, mimesis, and catharsis that defined the functioning of this new paradigm.

Obviously, all this did not escape the classical-record industry, particularly at Deutsche Grammophon. The disappearance of the great historic conductors of the latter half of the twentieth century would soon allow the artistic directors to take the pulse of the new empirical reality. The notable personalities who had defined, with such intelligence, the principles of Apollonian neoclassicism were, in fact, just on the point of retiring at that time: the great artistic director Günther Breest, the brilliant Andreas Holschneider, and the remarkable Pali Meller Marcovicz had, in the space of five years, left their posts, one after the other, creating a huge void at the Hamburg headquarters. The teams that succeeded them carefully weighed the necessity of designing a new type of cover in keeping with the evolving Dionysian revolution, or even preempting it so as to better control its effects.

This proved all the more essential as the focus on the performer had intensified, giving rise to international productions receiving tremendous media coverage, such as the Berlin Concert with Plácido Domingo, Anna Netrebko, and Rolando Villazón, or Pavarotti and Friends, which multiplied and made crossovers commonplace. Furthermore, the Dionysian paradigm has directed the record industry toward a new public, which better corresponds to its world: young people. This has further reinforced the parallel of the visual communication of media celebrities of all kinds with that of the opera singer.

In this context, the composition of Deutsche Grammophon's covers could only evolve in the same direction, and the modifications have been conspicuous. The cartouche has been reduced to a far more modest size, and its placement is no longer determined by an invariable structure but instead depends solely on its graphic interaction with the photo of the artist, which currently occupies the entire cover. Information about the work(s) is no longer inside the cartouche but directly on the photo. Its location and size are also determined case by case, depending on the selected photo.

The image itself is centered much more on the performer and his or her contact with the buyer. Whereas interaction between the artist in the photograph and the consumer had previously been almost nonexistent to underscore the distance, it is now the staging, the artist's charm, or a studio portrait that create a direct relation with the public. And showing off the performer's appearance to advantage sometimes plays an important role in generating sought-after media coverage. It should, however, be noted that this is not the case with certain artists who established their communication style in the era of Apollonian neoclassicism; artists such as Claudio Abbado or Maurizio Pollini, whose images remain governed by the earlier principles.

Of course, all of the aforementioned formal evolutions do not, in any way, point to a change in artistic or technical standards; but they do bring out an undeniable recent change in the artist's presentation and image. These reflect a profound upheaval of traditional graphic codes, justified by the joint desire of the record industry and the new generation of artists that it is promoting to decompartmentalize classical music and make it more accessible to the great majority. As Andreas Holschneider confirms, "Things have changed, as artists want to be liked by young people, and numerous young artists and musical groups have joined Deutsche Grammophon. They all want access to the youth audience, and the young are looking for a new kind of relationship with these artists. Consequently, it seems to me that building the image of an artist as we did twenty or thirty years ago would be a mistake." Which goes to show that the history of the image in the classical-record industry is not any more permanent than in other cultural productions, which are still rooted in their own era, even though they incorporate elements from the past.

DR. HANS HIRSCH
Former Artist and Repertoire Director, Deutsche Grammophon

You joined Deutsche Grammophon in 1954 as a product manager in charge of Archiv Produktion, then became the assistant to the Yellow Label's A&R department director, Otto Gerdes, before succeeding him between 1970 and 1982. You were then appointed vice president of PolyGram, in charge of Recording Operations, from 1982 until 1985. Was it easy for Deutsche Grammophon to work with international artists in the 1950s in the aftermath of the Second World War?

During the first years after the Second World War, Deutsche Grammophon mainly worked with German artists, or with German-speaking artists from Austria and Switzerland. In the early 1950s Elsa Schiller came from RIAS (the broadcasting station in the American sector of Berlin) to Deutsche Grammophon. Born in Hungary as a Jew and forced to live in the concentration camp at Theresienstadt, she was able to counteract any insinuated connection between Deutsche Grammophon and Germany's Nazi past. Excellent personal relationships within the classical musical world helped her to make Deutsche Grammophon attractive for artists from any country, though there was a certain focus on Hungarian and Swiss artists (Ferenc Fricsay, Géza Anda, and Maria Stader), in addition to the German and Austrian ones (Wilhelm Furtwängler in his very last phase, Karl Böhm, Eugen Jochum, Wilhelm Kempff, and Wolfgang Schneiderhan). Simply, you could say that during the 1950s, Elsa Schiller developed Deutsche Grammophon from a German to a European company, where artists appreciated the more natural sound of the Deutsche Grammophon recordings and the better pressing quality of their records.

How was the famous Yellow Label conceived?

As far as I know, Hans Domizlaff created it in 1949. In its dominant, large size, the cartouche, created in 1958, was used for high-price releases; in a smaller size and in changing positions, for mid-price and budget releases. It was a basic principle of the graphic design that the type for the artist's name was never to be larger than that used for the composer—except in the case of selections of different titles/composers performed by a special artist. Whether a picture of the composer, of the artist(s), or other artwork was selected depended on the respective program. The main objective, of course, was to persuade the public to "buy this record!" This aim certainly has not changed, even though the aesthetic approach may have altered since then.

What kind of artistic policy did you want to implement yourself?

During the 1960s, developments of the 1950s were continued so that what had been a European company became a truly international one, in which A&R activities ran parallel to Deutsche Grammophon's marketing and sales organizations under the guidance of Kurt Kinkele. Now even more recordings were made in the UK, France, Italy, and the USA, and major artists were also signed from the USA (for example, an exclusive contract was signed with the Boston Symphony Orchestra). New repertoire lines were also launched, such as *avant garde* and *Debut*. When I became A&R director in 1970, I simply wanted to continue, to expand, and to strengthen such growth.

Looking for the most promising young artists was always considered to be of paramount importance at Deutsche Grammophon; as important as the cultivation of Deutsche Grammophon's relations with its established artists. Martha Argerich, Christoph Eschenbach, and Maurizio Pollini were almost unknown when they made their first recordings for Deutsche Grammophon; Claudio Abbado, Seiji Ozawa, and Carlos Kleiber were known only to a few experts back then. Anne-Sophie Mutter is perhaps the most prominent example of a performer whose development from a girl in her early teens to a great and mature artist was continuously encouraged and meticulously promoted, thanks especially to the artistic support given by Herbert von Karajan. Such successes were achieved by permanently observing the musical "market," which meant making countless trips to concerts, opera performances, and competitions, and fostering connections between young artists and established stars.

You produced a lot of LPs with Herbert von Karajan. Could you describe the "Karajan sound?"

My early musical experiences were strongly influenced by what could be called the old German tradition, and by conductors, such as Furtwängler, Jochum, Keilberth, and Knappertsbusch. So I was impressed by Karajan's interpretation of Beethoven, with the perfect playing of the Berlin Philharmonic, full sfumato sound and his elegant conducting gestures, but I had some problems with his aesthetic concept (particularly his tempos and tempo relations) when I first heard him in a live concert around the mid-1950s. It was not until almost ten years later that he really enthralled me with Debussy's *La Mer*, with incredibly differentiated sound colors and dynamic nuances. Michael Gielen, who in the early 1950s was one of Karajan's assistants at the Vienna State Opera (and certainly not likely to have idolized him), remembers in his recently published autobiography, *Unbedingt Musik* (Insel Verlag, 2005), a Wagner rehearsal at La Scala in Milan, where he had to prepare the orchestra for the Maestro: "When he appeared for *Tristan*, he started with the third-act prelude, stopped after the first phrase and mumbled something that, I swear, nobody was able to understand. Then they played once more—and it was a transformed orchestra; the 'Karajan sound' was there, a sound I could talk about but not re-create. This magic power with the musicians…was his genius." I feel unable to describe my own impressions in a better way (and not only with regard to Karajan's Debussy).

How do you explain the extraordinary success of Karajan during all those years?

In 1963 Karajan's new recordings of the complete Beethoven symphonies with the Berlin Philharmonic were released, for the very first time in record history sold by subscription (a scheme initiated by Kurt Kinkele): eight LPs in a luxurious box together with a detailed booklet. Between 700,000 and 800,000 sets were sold (in other words about 6,000,000 LPs) in just a few months! This level of sales was, until then, totally unknown in the international classical music business, and it had a huge impact on sales of his other records as well. Deutsche Grammophon was faced with the major task of preventing other musicians from feeling neglected as a result of this success.

You brought Carlos Kleiber to Deutsche Grammophon. Why did he record only a few LPs?

Certainly Carlos Kleiber was a very special artist. When I first approached him and asked him about his aspirations regarding the repertoire, he answered—and meant it—quite honestly, consciously and openly, "*Jede nicht aufgenommene platte ist eine gute platte*," which means something like "Each unrecorded record is a good record." As I subsequently heard him express this sentiment many times, I was—and still am—really proud of having been able to entice him to make all of his (rare) legal recordings, except one, for Deutsche Grammophon.

According to you, what were the main characteristics of Deutsche Grammophon's catalogue?

Deutsche Grammophon has always strived for a balance between the various musical genres—operas and choral music, symphonic and concerto repertoire, and chamber music (solo and ensemble, instrumental and vocal). Each musical period had to be sufficiently represented. While Archiv Produktion focused especially on pre-classical music, the Yellow Label concentrated on music from the Viennese classics via the Romantic composers to contemporary composers (particularly Stockhausen and Henze). Several more or less complete editions have to be mentioned: in 1970, the archetypal *Beethoven Edition* (to commemorate the 200th anniversary of the composer's birth); in 1973 (Deutsche Grammophon's 75th anniversary), *The World of the Symphony* (ten boxes with the complete symphonies of nine composers from Mozart to Mahler—only Haydn limited to his twelve *London* symphonies—and, with the exception of Sibelius and Tchaikovsky, each composer performed by a single conductor); in 1983 the complete *Brahms Edition* (for his 150th anniversary), consisting of all works with opus numbers written by this important composer, plus a selection of his other works. Based on systematic A&R ideas and schedules, such comprehensive releases can unquestionably be regarded as one of Deutsche Grammophon's major achievements.

How would you describe the evolution of the classical-music industry from the 1960s to the present time?

Without doubt, the record industry as a whole has suffered a lot from the widespread free availability of its products on the Web. Although, certainly, pop repertoire has been hit even more severely, I think that classical music—although it represents only a small percentage of the turnover of the music industry as a whole—cannot be left untouched by such general decline. Apparently, events—of whatever kind (think of the Three Tenors)—have taken precedence, with an even stronger emphasis placed on artists than on repertoire, and many attempts have been made at combining pop and classical elements with so-called crossovers. An important objective, both today and for the future, is to create and reinforce an interest in classical music in the younger generation (remember Bernstein's Young Peoples' Concerts), as well as considering how to secure an audience for so many extremely gifted young artists.

MICHAEL LANG
President of Deutsche Grammophon

You were general manager of Deutsche Grammophon from 2001 to 2006 and since then have been its president. Why did you wish to celebrate Deutsche Grammophon's 111th anniversary?
Well…it certainly would have been more usual to have celebrated our *110th* anniversary; however, 2008 was also Herbert von Karajan's 100th anniversary, and we did not think it appropriate or feasible to celebrate two significant anniversaries in the same year. Therefore, as the artist has always come first, we deferred our Deutsche Grammophon celebration for one year. However, the point here—be it 110, 111, or 211 years—is to share our pride and joy that Deutsche Grammophon remains the preeminent classical-recording company, alive and kicking after 111 years.

What does Deutsche Grammophon mean to you?
From childhood memories of my father's LP collection (which extensively featured Deutsche Grammophon albums), to selling many Deutsche Grammophon discs during the twenty years that I worked in and owned retail record shops, to becoming a marketing manager for PolyGram Classics & Jazz in the early 1990s, and finally to working at Deutsche Grammophon itself, this label has always been the epitome of classical music recording—it is my great fortune to be part of the most important classical-record company in history.

How would you describe the artistic policy of these past ten years?
To nurture the artistic vision and to develop the careers of our iconic artists, and to discover the next generation of great artists—all by producing recordings of the highest artistic and technical standards and then creating the most attractive album artwork and compelling reasons for the classical music enthusiast to buy them.

A new generation of artists (Anna Netrebko, Elīna Garanča, Magdalena Kožená, Rolando Villazón, Patricia Petibon, and Gustavo Dudamel, among others) has emerged. What do they bring to the repertoire?
What is interesting about classical music and recording (and, unfortunately, misunderstood by many outside observers) is to listen to and compare a musician's interpretation of a repertoire with those of his or her peers as well as predecessors—what these young artists bring to us is that fresh perspective, as well as extending and redefining the tradition of this art.

It seems obvious that Deutsche Grammophon has decided to modernize, to refresh the relationship between its artists and the audience. Thanks to the Internet, a closer proximity to the public has been possible. Why did you choose this option?
As Deutsche Grammophon has continually been at the technological forefront of the recording business, I do not see our foray into the digital world as anything different from what Deutsche Grammophon has always done—and by creating our own Web shop, we are able to ensure that our artists' music reaches their audience in the best digital-audio quality possible. I do not

think the buyer of any Deutsche Grammophon recording expects any less. If people are now going to purchase their music via the Internet, then Deutsche Grammophon quality has to be there, too.

How is it possible to remain a leader in the classical music industry—that is to say, an industry based on tradition, history, and high standards, where masterpieces are recorded to last—in a global market dominated by products with a short shelf life?
It is true that we have become a disposable society in many ways; however, not in every way. I am confident that fine art—in any medium—will and must continue to hold a place in our cultural society. And so we maintain our standards.

Do you think that classical music has a broader and more diverse audience than twenty or thirty years ago?
I believe that developing a new audience, a new generation, for *all* of the arts (including, of course, classical music!) is not only Deutsche Grammophon's great concern, but also, I hope, of great concern to our society.

How do you see the development of Deutsche Grammophon's strategy over the next decade?
While our artistic strategy remains as strong as ever, we all know that the recording business has become quite challenging: the price of producing great recordings must be compensated for by the income they generate—and it is not clear that the old, simple formula can work within this new marketplace. Therefore Deutsche Grammophon, with the support of its parent company Universal Music's classical division (also including Decca Records), is expanding its classical music activities into artist management, concert production, television production, and music publishing—as well as creating partnerships with businesses, in fields other than classical music, to underwrite the cost of recording classical music. These additional activities already help support and sustain Deutsche Grammophon's role as *the* music-recording company.

CLAUDIO ABBADO

Photo: Harald Hoffmann / DG

It has been a pleasure to have collaborated with Deutsche Grammophon since 1967. From the start, this experience has been enjoyable: imagine what it's like to begin one's relationship by recording the Prokofiev and Ravel piano concertos with Martha Argerich and the Berliner Philharmoniker! And now, for more than forty years, we have maintained this outstanding relationship—based on common aesthetic, artistic, and technical aims. During these four decades, Deutsche Grammophon committed itself to make great recordings with Beethoven, Brahms, Mahler, and Schubert cycles—as well as Mozart's major operas. It is a wonderful opportunity for an artist to record for Deutsche Grammophon, not only because of its unparalleled history but for its artistic excellence. I've witnessed its continual support for both musicians and for outstanding orchestras, such as the Berliner Philharmoniker, as well as for new orchestras, such as the Mozart Orchestra, with which we have recently recorded Mozart's late symphonies and Pergolesi's sacred masterworks—I have deeply enjoyed working with such passionate professionals, devoted to their cause and sharing common ambitions to serve music, musicians, and repertoire. Happy Anniversary, Deutsche Grammophon!

ROBERTO ALAGNA

Photo: Alix Laveau / DG

My first recording on the famous Yellow Label was somewhat anachronistic: Luis Mariano. It marked the beginning of a new adventure in my career that crossed over the borders of opera. I arrived on this label with projects that were totally different from anything that I had done until then. And the team at Deutsche Grammophon gave me, and gives me every day, the freedom to carry them out, with their complete confidence.

It was in this climate of trust and working harmony that I was able to record the disc *The Sicilian*, a popular repertoire that no classical, or even pop singer, was interested in doing until then. Deutsche Grammophon took the risk with me without hesitation. And I am even happier that, as we've seen, these albums have been so enormously successful with the public. This was also the case with the birth of *Le Dernier Jour d'un Condamné* ("The Last Day of a Condemned Man"), the opera written by my brothers David and Frédérico, based on Victor Hugo's novel. The work was premiered in Paris in July 2007, where it was recorded live, and was released in the following months. For me, this commitment is the daily proof of trust and generous support. In popular repertoire as well as in classical, I receive help from a team who is ready to defend my choices.

The DVD has always occupied a major place in my discography, and Deutsche Grammophon didn't hesitate to distribute Alfano's *Cyrano*, an opera that was more or less unknown at the time, nor Leoncavallo's *Pagliacci*. I have also been very honored that all my recordings from previous recitals have been taken up by this very prestigious company and integrated into its catalogue to be distributed all over the world.

Deutsche Grammophon has supported me in all my desires, and has listened to me and given me attention on a daily basis. And the adventure continues.

RAFAŁ BLECHACZ

Photo: Felix Broede / DG

My first contact with Deutsche Grammophon was a Christmas present I received eighteen years ago: Beethoven's *Pastoral* Symphony, with Leonard Bernstein conducting the Vienna Philharmonic. I already had a pretty big classical collection when I was a first-year music student, and I soon realized that the recordings I chose and enjoyed listening to most often had a yellow cartouche. That logo told me to expect the highest artistic quality, to expect excitement and emotion from the music on those yellow-labeled records. Today, I am happy and grateful to be one of the Deutsche Grammophon artists celebrating 111 years of its history. This three-digit number is a triple confirmation of the company's fidelity to classical music, its professionalism, and its willingness to share the beauty of art with millions of music lovers all around the world. I also firmly believe that Deutsche Grammophon's respect for tradition and never-ending quest for perfection will ensure that these words remain true 111 years from now.

PIERRE BOULEZ

Photo: Felix Broede / DG

Ever since my recording of *Parsifal* in 1970, Deutsche Grammophon has played a central role in the preservation, promotion, and distribution of my interpretations. The disc has played an indispensable role in documenting music spanning the whole of our century. It prolongs the moment of real listening in a concert, or even replaces it, if conditions do not favor a direct encounter with the music. Deutsche Grammophon has played, and continues to play, a fundamental role in the dissemination of twentieth-century works, and encourages this repeated link between live performances and recordings, which is so important in gaining familiarity with important compositions of the recent past and present. Without this precious assistance, our culture would be much impoverished.
With all my best wishes for a happy future.

PLÁCIDO DOMINGO

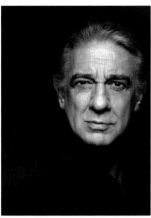

Photo: Dario Acosta / DG

In the world of classical music, Deutsche Grammophon's Yellow Label has long been acknowledged as a symbol of high quality, and it still is today. My own relationship with the company, although not exclusive, has been an extremely productive one, and has been going on for about 40 percent of Deutsche Grammophon's 111-year history!

As I think back on some of my Deutsche Grammophon recordings, I automatically recall the outstanding conductors I've worked with. I have particularly good memories of recording Beethoven's Symphony no. 9 with Karl Böhm, *Turandot* with Herbert von Karajan, *Die Meistersinger* with Eugen Jochum, *Oberon* with Rafael Kubelik, *La Traviata* with the unforgettable Carlos Kleiber, *Carmen* with Claudio Abbado, *Samson et Dalila* and the Berlioz Requiem with Daniel Barenboim, and *Nabucco* and *Tannhäuser* with Giuseppe Sinopoli. Or I think of all the wonderful Deutsche Grammophon Metropolitan Opera DVDs with James Levine—*Aida*, *Otello*, *La forza del destino*, *Simon Boccanegra*, *Manon Lescaut*, and *Turandot*—not to mention all the CDs that Jimmy and I have done together for Deutsche Grammophon: *Idomeneo*, *Parsifal*. Then there was the special project of recording all of Verdi's tenor arias, and releasing the set in 2001 to mark the 100th anniversary of the composer's death.

All in all, it has been and continues to be a very fruitful relationship!

EMERSON STRING QUARTET

Photo: Mitch Jenkins / DG

Eugene Drucker for the Emerson String Quartet
Before we became Deutsche Grammophon artists in 1987, and in the twenty-two years since, we have always thought of Deutsche Grammophon as the pinnacle of achievement in the classical-recording industry. We were thrilled when we learned of Deutsche Grammophon's interest in us; it was an honor to be included among the legendary musicians on its roster. Having recorded a great deal of the magnificent string quartet repertoire, and quintets with such artists as Mstislav Rostropovich, Menahem Pressler, and Leon Fleisher, we feel that our relationship with Deutsche Grammophon has represented a major part of our career and will form an even greater part of our legacy.

We have several wonderful memories of our longstanding and continuing relationship with Deutsche Grammophon: signing our first contract; winning our first Grammy and our first *Grammophon* Award for the Bartók quartets (when Deutsche Grammophon flew us from New York to London and back on the Concorde because we had a concert in the US on the same day as the awards ceremony in London); the concert and recording sessions for the Schubert quintet with "Slava," which were made possible by a partnership between BASF and Deutsche Grammophon; and recording all of the Shostakovich quartets during live concerts at the Aspen Festival, which yielded an additional two Grammys. There are more highlights in our recording career, too numerous to mention, but we have also always enjoyed our visits to company headquarters in Hamburg.

GUSTAVO DUDAMEL

Photo: Pierre-Henri Verlhac

Deutsche Grammophon has given me and the Simón Bolívar Youth Orchestra of Venezuela incredible opportunities and encouragement. Thank you, Deutsche Grammophon, and congratulations on another milestone anniversary.

DIETRICH FISCHER-DIESKAU

Photo: Mat Hennek / DG

It started with Elsa Schiller, director of the classical music division of the RIAS Berlin (where I took part in many productions from Schütz to Hugo Wolf), who then moved to the still-young Deutsche Grammophon. My first recording was of the quartet from the third act of *La Bohème* and, apart from my nervousness, I had not the slightest idea how many titles would follow this recording of September 19, 1949.

By then, I had met Maestro Ferenc Fricsay, who was quite surprised to find an Italian baritone in Berlin, and especially one who conducted the first recording of scenes from *Carmina Burana* by Carl Orff. Everybody, the RIAS Symphony Orchestra included, was enthusiastic about the new conductor in chief of the Städtische Oper Berlin, and Elsa Schiller was certainly the driving force behind the West Berlin classical music scene. We all had her to thank for bringing us this passionate and professional conductor.

The other piece of luck for me was becoming friends with Hertha Klust, who did so much for me by introducing me to most of the important lied literature from December 1949 onward. Another important conductor, Karl Ristenpart, was responsible for recording Bach cantatas, which gave Deutsche Grammophon a new image and opened the way to a broader interest in Bach's music. Operatic and important orchestra recordings with Fricsay and Artur Rother followed, and Fricsay, in particular, revived Berlin's musical life.

I was more than lucky to find Jörg Demus, an accompanying pianist for many, many lieder (Beethoven, Schubert, Schumann, Brahms, Wolf, Strauss, and many others), who seemed to please Elsa Schiller immensely and with whom I went on many tours.

It is impossible to name all of the conductors who have influenced me in my professional career: Böhm, Bernstein, and Maazel, to name just a few; and every one of them, each with his individual character, has had a great impact on me.

To Deutsche Grammophon, I am forever grateful that my recording plans could include practically the whole younger generation of Germans, above all Hans Werner Henze and Aribert Reimann, whose *Lear* was a considerable commercial and artistic success. Deutsche Grammophon represents to me—and to the music industry—an ideal platform for recording in the classical arena, as well as a source of plenty of new ideas in the field of current productions. May this distinguishing feature continue to make the difference!

Photo: Steven Haberland / DG

ELĪNA GARANČA

What does Deutsche Grammophon represent to you?
A guarantee of quality and a musical family which I feel very close to.

What is your best memory of Deutsche Grammophon?
My second solo CD, *Bel Canto*. It was a dream—a fantastic orchestra, conductor, and recording team—and there was such a good understanding and positive energy between us all.

What do you think is the distinguishing feature of Deutsche Grammophon?
Quite simply, Deutsche Grammophon has the finest artists in the world and the best professionals in the recording business. If you have only the very best, then the result will be the best, too.

Photo: John Sann / DG

OSVALDO GOLIJOV

Growing up in a small town in Argentina in the 1960s, I didn't have the experience of listening to great soloists or orchestras in concert. My earliest musical memories are of my mother playing the piano and the sounds from my parents' record collection, which consisted mainly of Deutsche Grammophon LPs. Those Deutsche Grammophon records were both my musical training and the gateway to a magic world of possibility in sound and drama.

My memories of discovering many masterpieces also include the record covers, the ever-present Yellow Label, and the exact moments when scratches and needle jumps occurred in the music, as well as turning the LP to side B as part of the ceremony. When listening to those records as a child, I was inside the house, in the world, but in another world as well. This form of ritual listening has changed with the arrival of new technologies, but I will cherish it forever, as a key experience of my early life, and one that has also shaped my future as an adult. I feel profoundly grateful for those memories, and honored that my music is now part of the Deutsche Grammophon world.

Photo: Mat Hennek / DG

HÉLÈNE GRIMAUD

As I sit here and reflect on what makes Deutsche Grammophon such a special record company, I realize that it's much more than an impressive history, tradition, and catalogue. I keep coming back to the people at the label who continue to carry the torch into the future so brilliantly and who make up a real family and creative home for so many of today's musicians.

As much as I would sometimes prefer to live in the past, in this case I'm convinced that what makes Deutsche Grammophon so remarkable is how everyone in that team today implements a strong and courageous vision—with total dedication of spirit and commitment to the cause and task at hand—always with great energy, not only physical and mental, but so often emotional as well. For that is truly what makes a difference: they engage their hearts so that the enthusiasm, adaptability, and vitality that define their work are not only productive but, most importantly, also create an atmosphere of artistic nurturing—a fertile and inspiring environment for us musicians. Congratulations on this remarkable anniversary and many happy returns.

Photo: Mathias Bothor / DG

HILARY HAHN

It is so rewarding to collaborate artistically with a company that has such a legacy of mutual respect and understanding with its artists. I have enjoyed every minute of my part in that legacy, and I'm honored to be connected with the company's illustrious name. May Deutsche Grammophon flourish another 111—or 222 or 333!—years to continue to make history.

DANIEL HOPE

Photo: Harald Hoffmann / DG

Ever since I was a child, the Yellow Label has been associated in my mind with the finest in music. Whether it was the majestic Karajan, the charismatic Bernstein, or the stylish Kempff, to name but a few, their "yellow" presence left an indelible impression on me from an early age, and their recorded legacy continues to be a source of constant inspiration to me. I never dreamed that one day I might be privileged to join the ranks of Deutsche Grammophon artists. I am thrilled to be a small part of such a unique and historic organization, among so many esteemed colleagues and legends. I am also happy to be recording at a time when we all look to the future of the industry to guide us through a new and exciting form of classical music recording and presentation. It goes without saying that Deutsche Grammophon will be at the forefront of this initiative for many years to come. I wish Deutsche Grammophon at least another 111 years of glorious, unabated music-making!

MAGDALENA KOŽENÁ

Photo: Mathias Bothor / DG

There are not many of us, lucky artists of my generation, who were given the extraordinary chance to get "married" to a major recording label so young. I am happy and proud to say that Deutsche Grammophon has been supporting me, challenging me and, as in every long-term relationship, occasionally driving me crazy, since the very beginning of my career.

Making recordings became, over these years, an essential part of my work; this is how I met many inspiring musicians and developed some of my most important collaborations (for example with Marc Minkowski and Andrea Marcon and their orchestras). I have always felt complete faith and freedom in everything I was doing, and I also appreciate the fact that, in spite of economically harder times, I was never pushed into a so-called "commercial project." I am grateful for any soul who (surely feeling from time to time like Don Quixote) cares and battles for classical music and its future. Thank you to everyone who makes these unique and special experiences happen. Happy Anniversary!

Photo: Olaf Heine / DG

LANG LANG

Deutsche Grammophon represents a wonderful tradition of making timeless music accessible to many people and preserving great interpretations for future generations. I admire Deutsche Grammophon because both of these things are of paramount importance to me as a musician and as a human being. In its 111 years, Deutsche Grammophon has managed to find a unique synergy between the traditional and the new. I felt this very strongly in all of our collaborations. I salute this amazing label and wish its team continued success and inspiration.

Photo: Anja Frers / DG

ANNE-SOPHIE MUTTER

In summer 1978 Deutsche Grammophon produced my first recording: Mozart's Violin Concertos no. 3 and no. 5 with Herbert von Karajan and the Berlin Philharmonic. This fulfilled a childhood dream for me—after all, the first LP I'd owned had been Anton Bruckner's Symphony no. 4 with Herbert von Karajan. To date, I have made another thirty-six recordings, including a whole range of first recordings, all of which represent what makes this label so inimitable—an absolute desire for top quality!

During the three decades of our international collaboration, the cultural and economic climate has changed dramatically. Many-a-great name from former times has disappeared from the CD shelves over the course of this period. In contrast, Deutsche Grammophon is celebrating its 111th anniversary. This is thanks to the ability of its employees and managers not only to react to new developments but also to anticipate them through strong and consistent innovation.

For me, Deutsche Grammophon's anniversary also expresses a particularly successful collaboration between artist and record label. I need a reliable and high-performing partner—not only in terms of production and marketing. It is also absolutely imperative for my survival that I can develop my repertoire in line with artistic criteria, without being suffocated by sales figures. I am, therefore, not only proud of my first recording with Deutsche Grammophon but also extremely thankful to "my" label.

I would like to congratulate the wonderful Deutsche Grammophon team on the occasion of this unrivaled anniversary—may they long continue to make the unheard accessible throughout the world!

Photo: Esther Haase / DG

ANNA NETREBKO

To me, Deutsche Grammophon represents everything that is great about recorded classical music. Growing up in Russia, I did not listen to many recordings at first, but once I began training to be an opera singer, I also started listening to recordings, and many of my favorite recordings are part of the Deutsche Grammophon catalogue. When I was asked to join the Deutsche Grammophon family, I felt incredibly honored and yet aware of the enormous responsibility of being part of that family.

I have many special memories of Deutsche Grammophon, but an outstanding moment was surely the recording of Russian arias that we made in St. Petersburg. It was wonderful to work with my mentor Valery Gergiev and his orchestra, and being able to show both my home country and my favorite Russian music to my friends at Deutsche Grammophon was a very special experience. What makes Deutsche Grammophon so unique is the amazing teamwork—from producers, technicians, and sound engineers to the marketing team. It is their commitment to their artists and their dedication to music that characterizes the entire Deutsche Grammophon team. I am very proud to be a part of celebrating this milestone of 111 years of Deutsche Grammophon—Happy Birthday, Deutsche Grammophon!

Photo: Felix Broede / DG

MARIA JOÃO PIRES

To me, Deutsche Grammophon represents a record company that sets the standard for classical music, so it meant a great deal to me when, at the age of forty, I first signed with them. To be accepted by that family of musicians gave me a very good feeling.

My best reminiscences of Deutsche Grammophon have to include recording the Schumann Concerto with Claudio Abbado. That was very special. Another special moment was when I signed my first contract in the old Vienna office with Aman Pedersen, and I still think very fondly of the first meeting I ever had with Dr. Holschneider and how he impressed me with his culture and vast knowledge.

The quality of the recordings on the Deutsche Grammophon label is always very high indeed. The expertise of the recording teams I have worked with has always been of the very highest order, and I have had the good fortune to work with the same Tonmeister (Helmut Burk) on most of my records.

Deutsche Grammophon has always provided excellent conditions in which to work (something not always found in the recording business), and I am most appreciative of the support and understanding I have received from the company during the many years of our collaboration.

MAURIZIO POLLINI

Photo: Mathias Bothor / DG

I have recorded for Deutsche Grammophon for nearly forty years. During this time we have documented a large part of my repertoire, including major works of contemporary music. I have always found the greatest professionalism in the people who collaborate with me—from executives to recording producers and technicians. I shall always be grateful to Deutsche Grammophon for enabling me to work under the best imaginable conditions.

Deutsche Grammophon Gesellschaft in all these years has played a highly important role in producing discs which, along with the most famous titles, also include important works that are not so popular—with a strong presence in chamber and early as well as contemporary music.

In the difficult current situation, nearly all of the recording companies and concert organizations find themselves confronted with an awkward decision: should they take the easier, more commercial path, based on easily marketable works? In my view, that would be a great mistake.

My wish is that the all-important role of these institutions in making all music available will continue in the future. I am convinced that despite the difficulties in the long run, that would be the more fortunate choice.

THOMAS QUASTHOFF

Photo: Felix Broede / DG

As far as I'm concerned, Deutsche Grammophon is the most eminent label for classical music that exists. Following the recording of Gustav Mahler's *Des Knaben Wunderhorn* with the Berlin Philharmonic, conducted by Claudio Abbado, I was offered an exclusive contract, the 10th anniversary of which was on May 10, 2009. This was the fulfillment of a dream for me. The fact that Deutsche Grammophon, a classical-record label, gave me the opportunity to release a jazz CD fills me with great joy and immense pride.

Photo: Mat Hennek / DG

VADIM REPIN

What does Deutsche Grammophon mean to you?
A fine team of people, who, despite the turbulent economic climate, are committed to producing core classical music recordings of uncompromised quality. At this stage of my life, Deutsche Grammophon is a great partner in my musical life.

What is your best memory of Deutsche Grammophon?
I have many, but one of them has to be the evening they organized for me in the Yellow Lounge in Berlin. A pioneering idea perfectly executed, and the memory of it will stay with me for a long time!

What do you think is the distinguishing feature of Deutsche Grammophon?
Tradition, leadership, quality—and no cheap crossovers!

Photo: Nicho Södling

ESA-PEKKA SALONEN

My first recollection of the Yellow Label was a Karajan recording of Sibelius's Symphony no. 4, which my father bought and proudly brought home one evening on his return from work. I cannot now remember his words exactly, but the gist was that this symphony was so strange and difficult to understand that he wanted to have a performance at a guaranteed high level and had, therefore, turned to Deutsche Grammophon.

Since then, the Yellow Label has been linked to uncompromising quality in my mind. And I'm delighted to say that now, several decades after my father's purchase (which was significant also for the fact that he usually browsed in secondhand record shops and tried to find bargains, but in this case happily paid the full price), I've had no reason to alter my perception of Deutsche Grammophon's commitment to core artistic values combined with a strong sense of adventure.

When I think of the label, not only do I think of the great old classic recordings by Karajan and Böhm (still my favorite recording of Bruckner's Symphony no. 7, and the live *Tristan* from Bayreuth 1966 is unsurpassed), but I also remember the excitement when all of those Stockhausen recordings were released. That was a truly important cultural event, and it is inspiring to see that the label has continued its commitment to new music ever since.

I have been a professional musician, a performer, and a composer for more than three decades now, and I thought there were few dreams left unrealized, but when I saw the first Deutsche Grammophon release of my own works, it felt special, like some kind of a milestone. To have one's own music alongside that of the old masters, on a label committed to the best, is an awesome and somewhat scary privilege.

BRYN TERFEL

Photo: Mat Hennek / DG

I was still at the beginning of my career when I made my first recording for Deutsche Grammophon, and not long after that, I signed an exclusive contract. The company and I have always had a wonderful working relationship. We've met every couple of months to talk about new projects—no label could be more open to its artists' wishes. For me, that's meant doing a huge variety of repertoire, because I try to embrace many musical styles. When I was keen to make a Wagner disc with Claudio Abbado and the Berlin Philharmonic, Deutsche Grammophon was only too happy to make that possible. And when I wanted to do an album of Lerner and Loewe, they were with me all the way. One couldn't ask for more from a record company. I look forward to many more years of this rewarding collaboration and wish Deutsche Grammophon all the best on its anniversary.

ROLANDO VILLAZÓN

Photo: Felix Broede / DG

My father worked in a recording company when I was a boy, and he used to bring a lot of LPs home with him. The recordings were mostly from the label he was working with (CBS) but occasionally there were also some from other labels. Whenever he brought home a Deutsche Grammophon LP, it somehow seemed to me that it weighed more. What made it heavier? Tradition, quality, art—and something else that I was not able to explain then. I felt that what I held in my hands (and heard in my ears) was not only an LP but also an artistic object, a little treasure.

The same elements that gave weight to LPs then continue to be present in the CD of today, but Deutsche Grammophon has also been alert and dynamic, and reacted to the challenges of modernity. It remains the label with the oldest and best tradition, but it is also the most modern classical label. Being part of Deutsche Grammophon is a big responsibility and has allowed me to understand that other element that I could not explain as a child: what makes Deutsche Grammophon the label it is are the people working there. All of them are knowledgeable, passionate, adventurous, and full of enthusiasm. To all of those who have built the great Yellow Label in these 111 years, I say "Congratulations," and to all of you whom I am lucky enough to work with, I say, from the bottom of my heart, "Thank you!"

SELECTED DEUTSCHE GRAMMOPHON ARTISTS

Listed once in alphabetical order by decade of first release

1898 - 1907
Sarah Bernhardt
Emma Calvé
Enrico Caruso
Feodor Chaliapin
Leopold Demuth
Emmy Destinn
Geraldine Farrar
Mary Garden
Alfred Grünfeld
Maria Gutheil-Schoder
Frieda Hempel
Josef Hofmann
Joseph Joachim
Karl Jörn
Paul Knüpfer
Jan Kubelik
Selma Kurz
Giuseppe de Luca
Nellie Melba
Alessandro Moreschi
Adelina Patti
Pol Plançon
Otto Reutter
Titta Ruffo
Chorus of the Teatro alla Scala, Milan
Antonio Scotti
Leo Slezak
Francesco Tamagno
Luisa Tetrazzini

1908 - 1917
Wilhelm Backhaus
Mattia Battistini
Berliner Philharmoniker
Michael Bohnen
Julia Culp
Claire Dux
Elena Gerhardt
Alfred Hertz
Lotte Lehmann
Richard Mayr
Arthur Nikisch
Ignace Jan Paderewski
Heinrich Schlusnus
Ernestine Schumann-Heink
Joseph Schwarz
Bruno Seidler-Winkler
Richard Strauss

1918 - 1927
Hermann Abendroth
Eugen d'Albert
Amar-Hindemith Quartet
Amar-Hindemith Trio
Rosette Anday
Leo Blech
Karin Branzell
Adolf Busch
Fritz Busch
Busch-Quartett
Gaspar Cassado
Mischa Elman
Carl Flesch
Oskar Fried
Wilhelm Furtwängler
Felicie Hüni-Mihacsek
Maria Ivogün
Hermann Jadlowker
Alfred Jerger
Wilhelm Kempff
Alexander Kipnis
Erich Kleiber
Otto Klemperer
Raoul von Koczalski
Fritz Kreisler
Georg Kulenkampff
Frida Leider
Emmi Leisner
Josef von Manowarda
Lauritz Melchior
Erica Morini
Maria Olszewska
Sigrid Onegin
Koloman von Pataky
Hans Pfitzner
Alfred Piccaver
Váša Prihoda

Walter Rehberg
Heinrich Rehkemper
Elisabeth Rethberg
Theodor Scheidl
Max von Schillings
Friedrich Schorr
Franz Schreker
Elisabeth Schumann
Staatskapelle Berlin
Staatskapelle Dresden
Josef Szigeti
Bruno Walter

1928 - 1937
Claudio Arrau
Erna Berger
Alexander Brailowsky
Willi Domgraf-Fassbaender
Dresdner Kreuzchor
Samuel Dushkin
Eduard Erdmann
Max Fiedler
Galimir String Quartet
Leopold Godowsky
Manfred Gurlitt
Robert Heger
Jascha Horenstein
Bronislaw Huberman
Paul van Kempen
Adele Kern
Bruno Kittel / Bruno Kittel-Chor
Hans Knappertsbusch
Tiana Lemnitz
Enrico Mainardi
Pietro Mascagni
Alois Melichar
Elly Ney
Julius Patzak
Julius Prüwer
Maurice Ravel
Wilhelm Rode
Helge Roswaenge
Chorus of the Staatsoper, Berlin
Igor Stravinsky
Wilhelm Strienz
Alexander Sved
Thomanerchor Leipzig
Viorica Ursuleac
Franz Völker
Hermann Weigert
Wiener Philharmoniker
Albert Wolff
Josef Wolfsthal
Alexander von Zemlinsky

1938 - 1946
Adrian Aeschbacher
Géza Anda
Eduard van Beinum
Helena Braun
Maria Cebotari
Concertgebouworkest
Gertrud (later Trude) Eipperle
Karl Elmendorff
Alfons Fügel
Christel Goltz
Josef Greindl
Hilde Güden
Horst Günter
Georg Hann
Heinrich Hollreiser
Hans Hotter
Herbert von Karajan
Margarete Klose
Viscount Hidemaro Konoye
Clemens Krauss
Annelies Kupper
Max Lorenz
Leopold Ludwig
Walther Ludwig
Georgine von Milinković
Maria Müller
Alda Noni
Gertrude Pitzinger
Victor de Sabata
Erna Sack
Hilde Scheppan
Carl Schuricht

Gino Sinimberghi
Li Stadelmann
Günther Treptow
Végh String Quartet

1947 - 1957
Amadeus Quartet
Karel Ancerl
Peter Anders
Stefan Askenase
Bamberger Symphoniker
Karl Böhm
Kurt Böhme
Kim Borg
Shura Cherkassky
Jörg Demus
Anton Dermota
Christoph von Dohnányi
Don-Kosaken-Chor / Serge Jaroff
Lorenz Fehenberger
Festival Strings Lucerne/Rudolf Baumgartner
Annie Fischer
Dietrich Fischer-Dieskau
Andor Foldes
Maureen Forrester
Ferdinand Frantz
Gottlob Frick
Ferenc Fricsay
Monique Haas
Ernst Haefliger
Clara Haskil
Paul Hindemith
Ludwig Hoelscher
Richard Holm
Janáček Quartet
Eugen Jochum
Julian von Karolyi
Margarete Klose
Koeckert-Quartett
Franz Konwitschny
Paul Kuen
Fritz Lehmann
Ferdinand Leitner
Leningrad Philharmonic
Hans-Martin Linde
Lorin Maazel
Igor Markevitch
Johanna Martzy
Josef Metternich
Evgeny Mravinsky
Gustav Neidlinger
Aurèle Nicolet
David Oistrakh
Igor Oistrakh
Sviatoslav Richter
Helmut Roloff
Hans Rosbaud
Leonie Rysanek
Paul Sacher
Kurt Sanderling
Wolfgang Sawallisch
Adolf Scherbaum
Anny Schlemm
Hans Schmidt-Isserstedt
Wolfgang Schneiderhan
Irmgard Seefried
Carl Seemann
Léopold Simoneau
Sir Georg Solti
Maria Stader
Rita Streich
Suk Trio
Elfriede Trötschel
Hermann Uhde
Tibor Varga
Astrid Varnay
Tamás Vásáry
Eberhard Waechter
Wiener Symphoniker
Wolfgang Windgassen
Fritz Wunderlich
Nicanor Zabaleta
Helmut Zacharias

1958 - 1967
Claudio Abbado
Maurice André
Martha Argerich

Martina Arroyo
Janet Baker
Ettore Bastianini
Siegfried Behrend
Carlo Bergonzi
Walter Berry
Inge Borkh
Thomas Brandis
Grace Bumbry
Lisa della Casa
Boris Christoff
Fiorenza Cossotto
Régine Crespin
José van Dam
Orchester der Deutschen Oper Berlin
Drolc-Quartett
Christoph Eschenbach
Brigitte Fassbaender
Christian Ferras
Rudolf Firkušný
Pierre Fournier
Agnes Giebel
Tito Gobbi
Friedrich Gulda
Hans Werner Henze
Heinz Holliger
Mieczysław Horszowski
Hungarian String Quartet
Gundula Janowitz
Sena Jurinac
Joseph Keilberth
Waldemar Kmentt
Klavierduo Kontarsky
Sándor Konya
Rafael Kubelik
Paul Kuentz
LaSalle Quartet
Evelyn Lear
Karl Leister
Pilar Lorengar
Christa Ludwig
Sir Charles Mackerras
Frank Martin
Jean Martinon
Edith Mathis
Martha Mödl
Gerald Moore
Edda Moser
Charles Munch
Birgit Nilsson
Rolando Panerai
Roberta Peters
Hermann Prey
Karl Ridderbusch
Anneliese Rothenberger
Orchestra del Teatro alla Scala
Paul Schöffler
Peter Schreier
Elisabeth Schwarzkopf
Renata Scotto
Tullio Serafin
Gérard Souzay
Janos Starker
Giuseppe di Stefano
Antonietta Stella
Thomas Stewart
Karlheinz Stockhausen
Gerhard Stolze
Teresa Stratas
George Szell
Giuseppe Taddei
Martti Talvela
Trio di Trieste
Tatiana Troyanos
Narciso Yepes
Karlheinz Zoeller

1968 - 1978
Salvatore Accardo
Theo Adam
Arleen Augér
Agnes Baltsa
Daniel Barenboim
Arturo Benedetti
Michelangeli
Teresa Berganza
Lazar Berman
Leonard Bernstein

Boston Symphony Orchestra
Pierre Boulez
Alfred Brendel
Leo Brouwer
Renato Bruson
Montserrat Caballé
José Carreras
Chicago Symphony Orchestra
Dino Ciani
Cleveland Orchestra
Ileana Cotrubas
Helga Dernesch
Plácido Domingo
Charles Dutoit
English Chamber Orchestra
Zino Francescatti
Mirella Freni
Sir James Galway
Sir John Eliot Gardiner
Nicolai Gedda
Emil Gilels
Carlo Maria Giulini
Barbara Hendricks
Marilyn Horne
Israel Philharmonic Orchestra
Carlos Kleiber
René Kollo
London Sinfonietta
London Symphony Orchestra
Loriot (Vicco von Bülow)
Los Angeles Philharmonic Orchestra
Melos Quartett
Sir Yehudi Menuhin
Sherrill Milnes
Nathan Milstein
Kurt Moll
Anne-Sophie Mutter
New Philharmonia Orchestra
Elena Obraztsova
Seiji Ozawa
Itzhak Perlman
Maurizio Pollini
Lucia Popp
Margaret Price
Steve Reich
Mstislav Rostropovich
San Francisco Symphony Orchestra
Heinrich Schiff
Ravi Shankar
Giuseppe Sinopoli
Hans Sotin
Frederica von Stade
Roberto Szidon
Michael Tilson Thomas
Tokyo String Quartet
Anna Tomowa-Sintow
Julia Varady
Krystian Zimerman
Pinchas Zukerman

1979 - 1988
Valery Afanassiev
Francisco Araiza
Kathleen Battle
BBC Symphony Orchestra
Hildegard Behrens
Barbara Bonney
Stanislav Bunin
Riccardo Chailly
Chamber Orchestra of Europe
Kyung-Wha Chung
Emerson String Quartet
Maria Ewing
Gothenburg Symphony Orchestra
Edita Gruberova
Jerry Hadley
Hagen Quartett
Matt Haimovitz
Thomas Hampson
Vladimir Horowitz
Neeme Järvi
Siegfried Jerusalem
Gidon Kremer
Philip Langridge
James Levine
Marjana Lipovšek
Witold Lutosławski
Yo-Yo Ma

SELECTED ARCHIV PRODUKTION ARTISTS

Listed once in alphabetical order by decade of first release

Mischa Maisky
Shlomo Mintz
James Morris
New York Philharmonic Orchestra
Jessye Norman
Leo Nucci
Orpheus Chamber Orchestra
Anne Sofie von Otter
Ivo Pogorelich
Ruggero Raimondi
Samuel Ramey
Jean-Pierre Rampal
Katia Ricciarelli
Matti Salminen
Andreas Schmidt
Trudeliese Schmidt
Rudolf Serkin
Gil Shaham
Giuseppe Sinopoli
Göran Söllscher
Cheryl Studer
Kiri Te Kanawa
Lucia Valentini Terrani

Ramón Vargas
Alberto Veronesi
Rolando Villazón
Yuja Wang
Franz Welser-Möst

1989 - 1998
Chorus and Orchestra of the Accademia
    Nazionale di Santa Cecilia
Juliane Banse
Cecilia Bartoli
Gianluca Cascioli
Sergiu Celibidache
Myung-Whun Chung
Augustin Dumay
Patrick Gallois
David Garrett
Andrei Gavrilov
Evgeny Kissin
Oliver Knussen
Roby Lakatos
Jean-Marc Luisada
Metropolitan Opera Orchestra & Chorus
Christiane Oelze
Orchestre de l'Opéra Bastille
Luciano Pavarotti
Maria João Pires
Michel Plasson
Mikhail Pletnev
André Previn
Christine Schäfer
Sting
Bryn Terfel
Christian Thielemann
Anatol Ugorski
Jian Wang
Lilya Zilberstein

1999 - 2009
Pierre-Laurent Aimard
Roberto Alagna
Ildebrando D'Arcangelo
Rafał Blechacz
Measha Brueggergosman
Diego el Cigala
Elvis Costello
Gustavo Dudamel / Simón Bolívar Youth
    Orchestra of Venezuela
Catrin Finch
Elina Garanča
Osvaldo Golijov
Hélène Grimaud
Ilya Gringolts
Hilary Hahn
Daniel Harding
Ben Heppner
Daniel Hope
Magdalena Kožená
Lang Lang
Yundi Li
Lucerne Festival Orchestra
Anna Netrebko
Orchestra Mozart
Alice Sara Ott
René Pape
Patricia Petibon
Thomas Quasthoff
Vadim Repin
Esa-Pekka Salonen
Mercedes Sosa

Late 1940s
Fritz Neumeyer
Edith Picht-Axenfeld
Helmut Walcha

1950s
Rudolf Baumgartner
Monks' Choir of the Benedictine Abbey
    Beuron / Maurus Pfaff
Dresdner Kreuzchor
Dietrich Fischer-Dieskau
Pierre Fournier
Ralph Kirkpatrick
Fritz Lehmann
Münchener Bach-Chor
Münchener Bach-Orchester
Pro Musica Antiqua / Safford Cape
Karl Richter
Schola Cantorum Basiliensis
Thomanerchor Leipzig
August Wenzinger
Fritz Wunderlich

1960s
Capella Academica Wien
Eduard Melkus
Regensburger Domspatzen
Ulsamer Collegium

1970s
Camerata Bern
Huguette Dreyfus
Early Music Consort of London
English Baroque Soloists
Sir John Eliot Gardiner
Kenneth Gilbert
Reinhard Goebel / Musica Antiqua Köln
Monteverdi Choir, London
Monteverdi-Chor Hamburg / Jürgen Jürgens
Monks' Choir of the Benedictine Abbey
Münsterschwarzach / Godehard Joppich
David Munrow
Trevor Pinnock / The English Concert
Konrad Ragossnig
Anna Reynolds
Nigel Rogers
Hanns-Martin Schneidt
Peter Schreier
Colin Tilney
Bruno Turner

1980s
Malcolm Bilson
Michael Chance
Choir of Christ Church Cathedral, Oxford
Robert Levin
Anne Sofie von Otter
Simon Preston
Simon Standage
Melvyn Tan
Choir of Westminster Abbey

1990s
Barbara Bonney
Michael Chance
Bernarda Fink
Gerald Finley
Rodney Gilfry
Magdalena Kožená
Paul McCreesh / Gabrieli Consort & Players
Sylvia McNair
Marc Minkowski / Les Musiciens du Louvre
Orchestre Révolutionnaire et Romantique
Orlando Consort
Piffaro - The Renaissance Band
Pomerium

2000s
Giuliano Carmignola
Concerto Köln
Alan Curtis
Simone Kermes
Andrea Marcon / Venice Baroque Orchestra
Viktoria Mullova

INDEX

CREDITS

1898–1945

[01]; [04]…[18]; [22]; [23]; [30]; [35]…[37]; [40]; [43]; [48]; [49]; [56];
[57]; [59]; [61]; [68]…[70]; [65] DG
[02] PrismaArchivo / Leemage
[03] Gusman / Leemage
[19] Selva / Leemage
[20] Rue des Archives / PVDE
[21] Lebrecht / Rue des Archives
[24] Joseph Martin / AKG Images
[25] Fototeca / Leemage
[26]; [27] Private collection / DG
[28] Lebrecht / Rue des Archives
[29] Jean Bernard / Leemage
[31] Mary Evans / Rue des Archives
[32]…[34] AKG Images
[38] Lebrecht / Rue des Archives
[39] Delius / Leemage
[41] AFC / Leemage
[42] Lebrecht / Rue des Archives
[44]…[46] Lebrecht / Rue des Archives
[47] AKG Images
[50] Max Treder, Charlottenburg / DG
[51] Rue des Archives / BCA / CSU
[52]…[54] AFC / Leemage
[55] Süddeutsche Zeitung / Rue des Archives
[58] AFC / Leemage
[60] Rights reserved
[62] AKG Images
[63] AFC / Leemage
[64] Edimedia / Rue des Archives
[66] Archives Decca
[67] Private collection / DG

1945–1979

[01]; [03]; [05]; [08]; [10]; [11]…[13]; [15]; [18]; [19]; [20]; [22];
[33]; [35]…[37]; [39]…[45]; [47]; [48]; [51]…[55]; [58];
[60]…[65]; [67]; [71]; [72]; [73]; [75]; [76]; [86]…[88]; [83]; [84];
[90]; [78]…[81]; [92]…[96]; [100]; [104]…[107]; [110]; [111];
[115]…[117]; [199]…[122]; [124]…[128]; [130]; [131]; [134];
[139]; [142]; [144]; [137]; [146]; [149]; [150]; [153]; [155]; [157];
[158]; [161]…[165]; [167]; [168]; [171]; [172]; [174]; [180]; [182];
[176]…[178] DG
[02] Photo-Lill
[04] Pierre-Henri Verlhac
[06] Siegfried Lauterwasser
[07] Lebrecht / Rue des Archives
[09] Max Jacoby
[14] Siegfried Lauterwasser
[16] Willy Saeger
[17] Lebrecht / Rue des Archives
[21] Jacques Schumacher
[34] Siegfried Lauterwasser
[38] Werner Neumeister
[46] Ruth Wilhelmi
[49] D. Heyden
[50] Private collection / DG
[56] Bruno Völkel
[57] Anthony Altaffer
[59] Fayer
[66] Rights reserved
[68] Werner Neumeister
[69] Hulton Archive / Getty Images
[70] Wien Fayer
[72] Pic / DG
[74] Werner Neumeister
[77] Arnold Newman / Getty Images
[82] Pic / DG
[85] Ilse Buhs
[89] Siegfried Lauterwasser
[91] Rights reserved
[97] Rights reserved
[98] Digne Meller-Marcovicz
[99] Piccagliani / Teatro alla Scala
[101]; [102] Werner Neumeister
[103] Siegfried Lauterwasser
[108] Ilse Buhs
[109] Kürt Jüliüs
[112] Anthony Altaffer
[113] Siegfried Lauterwasser
[114] Siegfried Lauterwasser / Unitel
[118] Private collection / DG
[123] Siegfried Lauterwasser
[129] Werner Neumeister
[132] Fritz von Swoll / Decca
[133] Siegfried Lauterwasser
[135]; [136] Werner Neumeister
[138] Private collection / DG
[140] L. Winkler
[141] Julian Hann
[143] G. MacDominic / Lebrecht / Rue des Archives
[145] Siegfried Lauterwasser
[147] Rights reserved
[148] Mali, Paris
[151] Mali, Paris
[152] MP / Leemage
[154] Siegfried Lauterwasser
[156] Alex «Tug» Wilson
[159]; [160] Siegfried Lauterwasser
[166] Gilda Hartmann
[169] Siegfried Lauterwasser
[170] Rights reserved
[173] Mike Evans
[175] Siegfried Lauterwasser
[179] Ken Veeder, Hollywood
[181] Clive Barda

1979–2010

[01]; [04]; [06]…[11]; [13]; [14]; [16]; [17]; [19]; [21]; [27]; [30]; [31];
[33]; [34]; [42]; [43]; [46]; [47]; [49]; [50]; [52]; [53]; [55]…[57]; [59];
[60]; [63]; [65]…[[67]; [69]; [70]; [72]…[74]; [76]…[80]; [83]; [86];
[87]; [89]; [91]…[93]; [99]…[103] DG
[02] Juri Gurewitchs
[03] Siegfried Lauterwasser
[05] Rights reserved
[12] Susesch Bayat
[15] Clive Barda
[18] Rue des Archives / ITAL
[20] Mike Evans
[22] Fred Fehl, 1959 Museum of the City of New York
[23] Susesch Bayat
[24] Siegfried Lauterwasser / Unitel
[25] Annette Lederer
[26] Arthur Umboh / DG
[28] Arthur Umboh / DG
[29] Denise Grünstein
[32] Stefanie Argerich
[35] Christian Steiner
[36]; [37] Clive Barda
[38] Marco Borggreve
[39] Harald Hoffmann
[40] Andreas Meyer-Schwickerath
[41] Siegfried Lauterwasser
[44] Photo-Schaffler
[45] Philippe Gontier
[48] Tug Wilson
[51] Susesch Bayat
[54] MP / Leemage
[58] Vivianne
[61] Malcolm Crowthers
[62] Mat Hennek
[64] Harald Hoffmann
[68] Jörg Reichardt
[71] Clive Barda
[75] Cordula Groth
[81] Clive Barda
[82] Charles Tandy
[84] Hugo Jehle
[85] Dan Porges
[88] Mathias Bothor
[90] Pierre-Henri Verlhac
[94] Rainer Maillard
[95] Felix Broede
[96] Mathias Bothor
[97] Steven Haberland
[98] Pierre-Henri Verlhac

FIFTY YEARS OF STEREO IN THE SERVICE OF MUSIC

[01]; [03]; [05]…[12]; [15]…[18]; [20]; [21]; [24]…[27]; [31]…[37];
[39]…[42]; [44]…[47]; [50]…[56]; [58]; [59]; [61]…[63];
[65]…[68]; [71]…[74]; [76]…[83]; [86]; [90]; [93]…[96];
[98]…[106]; [108]; [109] DG
[02] Ilse Buhs
[04] Max Jacoby
[13] Johnny Dirske / Decca
[14] Werner Neumeister
[19] Siegfried Lauterwasser
[22]; [23] Siegfried Lauterwasser
[28]; [29] Unitel
[30] Siegfried Lauterwasser
[38] Digne Meller-Marcovicz
[43] Irmgard Baeger
[48] Unitel
[49] Alex «Tug» Wilson
[57] Nigel Luckhurst / Lebrecht / Rue des Archives
[60] Rights reserved
[64] Fayer
[69]; [70] Siegfried Lauterwasser
[75] VEB Deutsche Schallplaten / Mirschel
[84] Siegfried Lauterwasser
[85] Christian Steiner
[91] Private collection / DG
[92] Philippe Gontier
[97] Philippe Gontier
[107] Klaus Lefèbvre

DEUTSCHE GRAMMOPHON'S VISUAL COMMUNICATION

[01]…[13] DG

ACKNOWLEDGMENTS
Listed in alphabetical order

We would like to thank Stephen Alpen, Lut Behiels, David
Butchart, Günther Breest, La Chaumière à Musique, Richard
Evidon, Ute Fesquet, Sophie Fetthauer, Marylise Hébrard, Bill
Holland, Michel Glotz, Daniel Goodwin, Hans Hirsch, Dagmar
Hoeck, Rainer Hoepfner, Andreas Holschneider, Alfred Kaine,
Eliette von Karajan, Elisabeth Koehler, Michael Lang, Richard
Laub, Reinhard Lüthje, Rainer Maillard, Ewald Markl, Philippe
Morin, Alan Newcombe, Philippe Pauly, Hocine Remadnia,
Hanno Rinke, Anja Rittmöller, Andrea Schroeder, Craig
Urquhart, Heinz Wildhagen, Bettina Wohlert, and all the artists
and their agents.

We would like to especially thank Thierry Soveaux for giving
access to his impressive Deutsche Grammophon record
collection.